JESUS WAS NOT CRUCIFIED

I. D. Campbell

I.D. Campbell

DEDICATION

This Book is dedicated to Yahya Luqman Saleem.

CONTENTS

IF YOU OPEN YOUR HEART AND YOU OPEN YOUR MIND, WHEN YOU READ THIS BOOK IT WILL OPEN YOUR EYES.

"A (retired) Christian minister for over 28 years. In all that time I had deep questions concerning the faith that I embraced. Of late, I read your book about whether Jesus was crucified or not and my mind rolled, my heart beat intensed, and my wondering about my private thoughts about the legitimacy of "The Trinity" have been intensified by your writing. I have your book in my computer, and will certainly scrutinized it. For the time being, your thoughts seem to parallel my own. Thank you." {This is an instant message received from a former Minster}

ACKNOWLEDGMENTS

First and foremost, ALHAMDULILLAH. ALL PRAISE IS DUE TO ALLAH. He is the source of all truth, therefore all that I convey of the truth in this book and in life are because of ALLAH, and only the mistakes are from me.

MY INTENTIONS

Al-Qur'an 4:157

That they said (in boast), "We killed Christ Jesus the son of Mary, the Messenger of Allah"; - but they killed him not, nor crucified him, but so it was made to appear to them, and those who differ therein are full of doubts, with no (certain) knowledge, but only conjecture to follow, for of a surety they killed him not:-

Al-Qur'an 4:158

Nay, Allah raised him up unto Himself; and Allah is Exalted in Power, Wise

These words are what Muslims believe to be the words of God revealed to Prophet Muhammad (pbuh). Because they believe these words to be the words of God, they are taken as absolute truth. Muslims do not believe that Jesus (pbuh) was killed or even crucified on the cross, but those who sought to kill him were under the impression that he was. It is interesting to note that the Qur'an differentiates between being killed and being crucified. Most people do not distinguish between the two. However it is possible to be crucified and not be killed. Both the Qur'an and the Bible agree on this point, which will be explained later. But the Qur'an states that he was not even crucified; that is to say, he was not affixed to the cross at all.

Of course, the Qur'an's claim is of little importance to those who do not believe it to be the words of God. Because it is not a biography of the life of Jesus (pbuh), this adds to the non-Muslim's contempt towards the Qur'an's declaration on this aspect of Jesus' (pbuh) life, which is almost universally accepted as a fact. However there exist four accepted biographies of Jesus (pbuh). What do they have to say about the events surrounding Jesus' (pbuh) supposed death? There are also several writings about Jesus (pbuh) in the New Testament. What do they say about the events surrounding Jesus' (pbuh) supposed death? Maybe more important to some people is the question, what is the reason for his death? I am, of course, a Muslim and it is apparent that I will be making an effort to show the validity of the Qur'anic understanding of Jesus (pbuh) and his supposed demise. I anticipate non-Muslims to be a bit cynical towards my explanations, but hopefully they will have an open mind when reading this book. I am drawing my conclusion from my reading and understanding of the scriptures. Every word that I type is my sincere belief. And it is not intended to offend, slander or mock anyone else's beliefs. My purpose is to have others to, at the very least, consider my argument.

I know that it is the prerogative of many people to immediately write off those who claim to read religious scripture with their own understanding, but I am convinced that one can arrive at the truth without having a degree in scripture [Remember Peter and John were disciples who were uneducated, common men. (Acts 4:13)] Higher learning will definitely enhance and advance your understanding, but if this is the criteria for the discovery of truth, then truth is in a world of trouble because only a handful of people will be able to arrive at truth, and only that handful will be qualified to articulate it to others. I believe the truth of religion will be established when there is a dialogue between those of different faiths. And this is my step towards that dialogue. I have no doubt that there will be scores of people who will believe my opinion to be totally erroneous or they may simply say that it is erroneous. But I only ask that those who do not accept my claims to present the alternative, so the people at large can decide for themselves which argument that they will believe. I have too often seen an entire book denounced with only a small amount of the material responded to. There is a huge difference between a "response" and a "refutation."

This book is very straightforward and fast paced. It contains a great deal of information, evidence and explanation. It is highly recommended that the reader have his/her Bible alongside them as they read. I quote and cite verses extensively from the gospels to prove my case, so I hope the reader takes the time to verify my findings step by step. Without checking the verses mentioned, the reader may assume that my conclusions are pure conjecture. I want the reader to read my book and the Bible and determine for themselves if my explanations are reasonable or if there is a better alternative to my findings. It may even be helpful to read the gospel accounts of Jesus' (pbuh) last days before and after reading this book to weigh the validity of my explanation.

It is extremely difficult to dispel a notion widely viewed as an axiomatic truth, if the person who holds this view is unfamiliar with the details of their belief. If you do not understand the Original Sin and atonement in Christianity and you are unfamiliar with the events surrounding Jesus' (pbuh) alleged death, it is probably unfair to have this book as your introduction to these subjects. If you are deficient in your knowledge about these subjects, I advise you to get your information from a source which is in support of these ideas. Therefore you are better equipped to evaluate my case against them.

With that said, I would first like to give the popular Christian view of the crucifixion of Jesus Christ (pbuh). Then I will give my views on the crucifixion and its purpose. In my explanation, I will be intentionally using the gospels as my primary source when discussing Jesus (pbuh) because they are purported to be the biographies of Jesus (pbuh). Jesus' (pbuh) actual actions and words are of greater consequence to me than the thoughts of people about Jesus' words and actions. In all honesty, I use this approach because Jesus' (pbuh) words and actions recorded in the four gospels are more favorable to my case than those of the other authors of the New Testament. This may seem like a weakness, but when this is put in proper perspective; my position will be the teachings "of" Jesus (pbuh) as opposed to the teachings "about" Jesus (pbuh). I intend to demonstrate that they are in sharp contrast to one another. If I am successful in this objective, those who believe in the crucifixion of Jesus (pbuh) cannot simply state that the Bible supports their case, a fact in which I will illustrate in the very first chapter, but they must show how Jesus' (pbuh) words correlate or corroborate their views. The fact that Jesus (pbuh) is a greater authority on his own teachings than anyone else is self-evident. Also, my explanation will be void of any references from the Qur'an until the very end of this book.

CHAPTER I – CHRISTIAN'S VIEWPOINT OF THE CRUCIFIXION

The Christian belief begins with Adam (pbuh) and Eve in the Garden of Eden. God told Adam (pbuh) that he can eat from any tree in the garden, except from the tree of knowledge of good and evil. God told Adam (pbuh) if he ate from this tree, that day he will surely die (Gen. 2:17). But Adam's (pbuh) wife, Eve is coerced by a serpent into eating fruit from the tree. The serpent told Eve that when she ate the fruit that she will not die, as God said, but she will be like God, knowing the difference between good and evil. So she ate the fruit and she gave some to Adam (pbuh) and he ate the fruit also. Because of this transgression, God punished them. When God confronted them, Adam (pbuh) blamed Eve for his sin and Eve blamed the serpent (Gen. 2:12-13). God cursed the serpent, which is considered to be the devil. (This conclusion is normally drawn from Revelations 12:9, which calls the devil, or satan, the old serpent which deceived the whole world.) Adam's (pbuh) punishment was that he was made to "sweat for bread" until he returned to the dust from which he was made. He was to work hard for food until his death. Eve was made to bear children in pain and to be ruled over by her husband for her sin. The Biblical viewpoint is that Eve was the person who should carry most of the burden.

__1Timothy 2:14__ And Adam was not deceived, but the woman being deceived was in the transgression.

However this is not all of the punishment. God told Adam (pbuh) if he ate from the tree, he would die. With this one transgression, Adam (pbuh) brought sin and death into the world. And this is not just physical death, but spiritually death or separation from God. This is understood from such verses as these:

__Romans 5:12__ Wherefore, as by one man sin entered into the world, and death by sin; and so death passed upon all men, for that all have sinned

__Romans 6:23__ For the wages of sin is DEATH

__Ezekiel 18:20__ The soul that sinneth, it shall die

Because of Adam's (pbuh) transgression, it is believed that all men are cursed to go to hell by God. This curse is called the Original Sin. This is not to be taken at face value as simply the first sin ever committed by man. The Original Sin is the fallen state of mankind because of his proclivity to sin. The first sin of Adam (pbuh) and Eve caused the Original Sin, a curse or stain upon every human being born. The Catholic Encyclopedia defines the Original Sin as "a consequence of this first sin, the hereditary stain with which we are born on account of our origin or descent from Adam."

Now this stain is on every human being. To make matters worse, man adds his own sins to the stain. Since every person is a sinner, it is incumbent upon man to find and kill an innocent sacrifice to atone for their sins. Before the birth of Jesus (pbuh), Christians believe the people of earlier times were obliged to use animal sacrifices to atone to God for their sins. But this kind of sacrifice was not enough, so when Jesus (pbuh) came to earth, he was the ultimate sacrifice. He was a completely sinless person, who willingly had himself killed to take away the sins of the world. And those who believe in him and his sacrifice will have ever-lasting life in heaven.

Romans 5:18 *Therefore as by the offence of one (judgment came) upon all men to condemnation; even so by the righteousness of one (the free gift came) upon all men unto justification of life.*

Romans 5:19 *For as by one man's disobedience many were made sinners, so by the obedience of one shall many be made righteous.*

It is attested by Christians that Jesus (pbuh) was persecuted, mocked, beaten and hung on a cross until he died. The gospels unanimously agree that Jesus (pbuh) gave up his ghost or his spirit on the cross (Matt. 27:50, Mark 15:37, Luke 23:46, John 19:30). Now it is incumbent upon everyone to accept his martyrdom as a great and noble act of love from God to have our sins forgiven.

John 3:16 *For God so loved the world, that he gave his only begotten Son, that whosoever believeth in him should not perish, but have everlasting life.*

Not only does the Bible say that Jesus (pbuh) was crucified, but that he was also resurrected from the dead three days after his crucifixion (Matt. 28:7, Mark 16:6, Luke 24:7, John 20:9). And he appeared to many people before he ascended to heaven to sit at the right hand of God.

Chapter II- REFUTATION OF THE CHRISTIAN VIEWPOINT

MY UNDERSTANDING

Since the Bible explicitly articulates the Christian's articles of faith, it seems a daunting task to embark upon an effort to disprove their faith using the same Bible. The reason, I think it can be done is because ever single aspect of their belief can not only be supported by the Bible, but it can be refuted by the Bible. In other words, I believe the Bible contradicts itself on a number of topics (a quick example: ***Proverbs 26:4*** *Do not answer a fool according to his folly...****Proverbs 26:5*** *Answer a fool according to his folly...*Which rule do you adhere to?) and more specifically the entire basis for the Christian belief in salvation. It becomes more fathomable when we realize that the Bible was written over a span of 1,500 years by over 40 different authors. How likely is it that that many authors could agree on every topic discussed in the volume of 66 books for the Protestants and 73 books of the Catholics? I will explore some of the inconsistencies in the narration of Jesus' (pbuh) last days in an effort to demonstrate that the story is not as straightforward as it has been taught to be. But first I must discuss Christians' understanding of Jesus (pbuh) and their salvation.

IS JESUS GOD?

Most Christians believe Jesus (pbuh) to be God. They believe that because he is God, he is the only person sufficient to be sacrificed for the sins of the world. I have dealt with the divinity of Jesus (pbuh) extensively in my book entitled "There Is No Trinity" and I feel that this book effectively eliminates the idea that Jesus (pbuh) is God. But I also recognize that there are Christians who believe in the crucifixion and totally or partially reject the divinity of Jesus (pbuh). For this reason, I will attempt to prove that Jesus (pbuh) was not crucified whether he was God, a man or whomever. But for those who believe Jesus (pbuh) to be God, I will provide a few thinking points.

First of all, Jesus (pbuh) had a God. On the cross, he called to his God to help him (Mark 15:34). His God was also greater than he was (John 14:28). And Jesus (pbuh) is not omnipotent (John 5:30) or omniscient (Matt. 24:36), yet his God is. This leaves you with the option of believing in more than one God, one with greater power than the other, or believing that Jesus (pbuh) was not God, but an agent and messenger of God. Since Christianity is a monotheistic religion, the latter option is what may better suit their need to reconcile the words of Jesus (pbuh) and the First Commandment proclaiming belief in one God.

To those who believe that Jesus (pbuh) is God, I would ask, "What is the possibility of pouring an ocean into a ballpoint pen?" It is impossible to do so, yet this is more plausible to believe than the claim that all the majesty, knowledge, and power of God was poured into a human body of any proportion. A human would cease to exist from the mere sight of God (Ex. 33:20). So how are we to understand that his weak mortal body can house the GREATEST, MOST UNIMAGINABLE POWER EVER? I am aware that many people concoct explanations to these problems, so I made it my duty to answer every possible explanation that I could imagine in the aforementioned book. But hopefully these examples will suffice to prove that Jesus (pbuh) is not God here.

Most Christians believe that Jesus (pbuh) had to be God to be a pure sacrifice. They say that it is not enough to just have a sinless man to die for our sins. In fact, they do not believe it is possible to be a sinless man because of the Original Sin, which is inherited in every child. If every person received this curse, then Jesus (pbuh) had the Original Sin, also. No Christian would agree to this, but it would explain Jesus (pbuh) going to John the Baptist to be baptized, because baptism washes away sin (Mark 1:4, 9). If you were to ask a Christian, "where is this stain or curse?" They probably would tell you that it is on your soul. Now you may ask, "where does the soul come from?" The answer, "From God." So God makes a spirit unholy and puts it into a child? Most people would be hesitant to say God makes unholy spirits. These kinds of questions have made Christian apologists rethink their answers. Many will say that the parents passed down the sin. And in order to clear Jesus (pbuh) from the Original Sin, it must be said that the father, not the mother, carries the stain. But then there arises the problem of Mary. Because God chose her to carry him in her womb, she too must be expunged from the list of those afflicted.

This necessity gives birth to the "Immaculate Conception" of Mary. The "Immaculate Conception" is the doctrine which says that Mary was born from divine grace without the Original Sin and she was immune to sin. I must note that neither of these ideas, "the Original Sin" or the "Immaculate Conception," was articulated by Jesus (pbuh) or his disciples, yet the Pope of 1854 made this an article of faith for Catholics.

"We declare, pronounce and define that the doctrine which holds that the Blessed Virgin Mary, at the first instant of her conception, by a singular privilege and grace of the Omnipotent God, in virtue of the merits of Jesus Christ (pbuh), the Savior of mankind, was preserved immaculate from all stain of original sin, has been revealed by God, and therefore should firmly and constantly be believed by all the faithful."

-Pope Pius IX, Ineffabilis Deus, 1854

Due to Mary's Immaculate Conception and Jesus (pbuh) miraculous birth, Jesus (pbuh) was free from the stain of the Original Sin. And he was considered to be sinless, thus Jesus (pbuh) met the criteria to be a sacrifice without having to be God. But most Christians say that a mere mortal man cannot eradicate sin from the world, only God can do this. However, when you ask them did God die on the cross, they will emphatically deny that God died. They say that only the human side of Jesus (pbuh) died on the cross, which brings us back to their claim that no man can die for sins. Because of this circular argument it is beneficial to disprove every aspect of their doctrine, step by step.

If the Original Sin Doctrine is not true, then the purpose of the crucifixion is void. And the crucifixion is of no effect, whether it happened or not. If the means of atonement for sins and God's forgiveness of sins given by Christians is not in agreement with the means of atonement and forgiveness in the Old Testament, then the act of crucifixion is again on no effect. If Jesus (pbuh) did not teach this idea of his demise for the atonement of sin for the world, then the act of crucifixion was merely a murder of a prophet. All these things will be established to show that even if he died on the cross, it has no bearing on man's salvation. And my ultimate claim is that the crucifixion was, in fact, a fiction, that has been misinterpreted and misunderstood by Christians and non-Christians for 2000 years.

DENOUNCING THE ORIGINAL SIN

Ecclesiastes 7:29 *Behold, this only have I found, that God made man upright; but they have sought out many inventions.*

Is this statement true or false? This verse alone contradicts the notion that God has punished mankind with a curse for the sins of Adam (pbuh) and Eve. To be more specific, God condemned mankind for the act of one person, Adam (pbuh) according to the Bible.

Romans 5:18 *Therefore as by the offence of one (judgment came) upon all men to condemnation...*

Romans 5:19 *For as by one man's disobedience many were made sinners...*

Is this the just and righteous God in whom we are to believe? One who curses everybody forever, for one sin of one person on one occasion? How exactly am I responsible for the sins of Adam (pbuh)? How are my children responsible for the sins of Adam (pbuh)? The question is rhetorical. It's obvious that we are not responsible in the least. But according to the Bible, Adam (pbuh) and Eve are not even responsible because they had to eat from the tree of knowledge in order to understand that they had sinned at all. Only after they ate the fruit did they understand good from evil (Gen. 3:22). And if they should have been punished at all, the punishment that they received should have been enough without involving the whole of humanity. There is no civilized nation on earth which punishes the children and the children's children and so on, forever for the crimes of one person, no matter how great the transgression of the law.

Solomon (pbuh) in his book called Ecclesiastes says that God has made man upright or righteous and that it is man who is does wrong. Man is not born into condemnation as Paul says in the book of Romans. According to Jesus (pbuh), children are born innocent (Mark 10:14, Matt. 19:14). In fact, the idea of being "born again" hinges on the premise that children are innocent and it is incumbent on people to digress to a childlike state of innocence in order to progress as a righteous adult.

This is the first example of conflicting stances on the same topic present in the Bible. One must decide which is the more logical and reasonable option. Which is more fair, righteous and just? You are born righteous and you corrupt yourself or you are born corrupted and condemned from the sins of your forefathers? It should be noted that the Jews, who have adhered to the principles of the Old Testament long before Christians accepted it as the words of God, have never accepted the idea of the Original Sin. Jews do not believe that you are born a sinner because of Adam (pbuh) and Eve, but that you are born pure and you chose to sin or not to sin. So, sin is not inherited from your parents.

Perhaps the early writers of the New Testament were confused by the numerous occasions in the Old Testament, in which descendants of a person are punished for the sins of their forefathers. That is to say, the sin or crime is not inherited but the punishment is inherited in the Old Testament. In terms of the Christian belief, it would mean that you do not inherit the sin nature from Adam (pbuh), but you will still go to hell for his sin, which is also unjust and unfair. In the Jewish Torah, we find that God punishes 10 generations of children for the fornication of two people (Deut. 23:2). God punishes up to fourth generations of people who hate him (Ex. 20:4). This is in sharp contrast to other verses in the Jewish Torah or the Old Testament, which totally absolve people for the sins of others, especially children for the sins of the parents. For example:

Jeremiah 31:30 Everyone will die for his own sin.

Deuteronomy 24:16 *The fathers shall not be put to death for the children, neither shall the children be put to death for the fathers: every man shall be put to death for his own sin.*

Isaiah 59:18 *According to their deeds, accordingly He will repay, fury to His adversaries, recompense to His enemies; to the islands He will repay recompense.*

Jeremiah 25:14 *For many nations and great kings shall make bondmen of them also; and I will recompense them according to their deeds, and according to the work of their own hands.*

Psalms 28:4 *Give them according to their deeds, and according to the evil of their endeavors; give them after the work of their hands; render to them their desert.*

The doctrine of the Original Sin is unacceptable in the light of these verses of the Bible. It is inconceivable that a just God would curse innocent people with sin or with the punishment of that sin. Those who believe in the Original Sin believe that the end justifies the means, but with God the means must justify themselves. The nobility of a person sacrificing himself for me, in no way, explains why or rectifies the fact that God cursed me in the first place for something I was not responsible for. I am inclined to believe in the Biblical stances that sin is not inherited and everyone is judged by and punished for their own deeds and misdeeds. Taking accountability for your own actions is a more just, fair, and righteous approach. It is also more just and fair to hold only the culprit responsible for his sins.

DISPROVING THE CHRISTIAN'S DOCTRINE OF ATONEMENT

1John 4:10 *This is love: not that we loved God, but that he loved us and sent his Son as an atoning sacrifice for our sins.*

Romans 5:8 *But God commendeth his love toward us, in that, while we were yet sinners, Christ died for us.*

Romans 5:9 *Much more then, being now justified by his blood, we shall be saved from wrath through him.*

These verses in a nutshell are what Christians believe to be the world's means of atonement for the Original Sin. Jesus Christ (pbuh) placed every born and unborn person's sin on his shoulders when he was killed on the cross. The first problem is that I have already established that the Bible says that man will be judged by his own deeds. So, it is logical to conclude that man will be punished for his own sins. Without, any references to scripture at the moment, is not this the more reasonable understanding of crime and punishment? If there is someone to take your punishment for you, is there someone who will reap the benefits of your good deeds, as well? The idea behind this kind of thinking is that God loves you so much that he had an innocent person, his own son, killed in order to save you. This is harped upon over and over, to such an extent that one does not second guess this notion. Is punishing an innocent person an act of love? And was it not God who condemned man in the first place for an inherit sin? In civilized society, we do not government in this way. We do not find the most innocent person and sentence him for the crimes of a mass murderer. And if a government did such a thing, we would look at them as barbaric and unjust, yet more than 2 billion people attribute such an injustice to God without the slightest reservations. We must realize that God is the judge, the jury, the prosecutor and the eyewitness. And he has absolutely no need to be unjust.

This Christian understanding of God's judgment is that of a judge who has found a person guilty of a crime, released him and punished his very own innocent son. Not to mention that the judge gave the person this criminal inclination. The implausibility of this act is completely apparent when we de-emphasize the sacrifice of the son, even if it is voluntary, and you analyze the case as a whole. Should not the guilty take the punishment or make the sacrifice? To illustrate my point further, there are ample verses of the Bible which illuminate this very sentiment.

Isaiah 55:7 *Let the wicked forsake his way, and the man of iniquity his thoughts; and let him return unto HaShem, and He will have compassion upon him, and to our G-d, for He will abundantly pardon*

Jeremiah 36:3 *It may be that the house of Judah will hear all the evil which I purpose to do unto them; that they may return every man from his evil way, and I may forgive their iniquity and their sin.*

Proverbs 16:6 *By mercy and truth iniquity is expiated; and by the fear of HaShem men depart from evil.*

2Chronicles 7:14 *if My people, upon whom My name is called, shall humble themselves, and pray, and seek My face, and turn from their evil ways; then will I hear from heaven, and will forgive their sin, and will heal their land.*

These verses totally destroy the claim that man is incapable of standing before God and gaining his own salvation and forgiveness from God through his repentance. All that God requires for forgiveness in these verses is man's sincere effort to eschew his past discretions. There is no mention of an intercessor or a mediator to help him to gain salvation or to lighten his burden. To further convey my understanding that each individual is responsible for his own deeds and each individual receives his own reward and punishment, I direct you to this verse.

Psalms 32:5 *"I acknowledged my sin unto thee, and mine iniquity have I not hid. I said, I will confess my transgressions unto the LORD; and thou forgavest the iniquity of my sin. Selah."*

Notice the "I's" in this verse. It shows personal accountability for one's actions.

ANIMAL SACRIFICE IN THE OLD TESTAMENT

Hebrews 9:22 *And almost all things are by the law purged with blood; and without shedding of blood is no remission.*

It is believed by Christians that Jesus' (pbuh) blood cleans the slate of sin for us all. This blood is the only means for forgiveness of sins. Christians deduce this from the practice of animal sacrifice to God performed and prescribed in the Old Testament. They contend that this kind of atonement is the way in which those who lived before Jesus (pbuh) walked this earth were accepted into heaven. However Christians maintain that these animal sacrifices were insufficient in purging the insurmountable acts of sins done by mankind, so God sent Jesus (pbuh) to be the sacrifice. But what does the Old Testament say about animal sacrifices? Christians often quote Leviticus 17:11 as a verse of the Jewish Torah which supports their position and at face value, it seems to do the job.

Leviticus 17:11 *For the life of the flesh is in the blood; and I have given it to you upon the altar to make atonement for your souls; for it is the blood that maketh atonement by reason of the life.*

It has been my experience that people become overzealous when reading about any topic concerning religion and they grab onto a verse or verses without considering its context. In a library of books as large as the Bible, it is possible to pull a few verses from any book to seem to agree with any idea you would like. That is why we must read the verse and considered the verses before and after them to determine if in fact they have the meaning that we wish to give it. One quick glance at the chapter and we find from the verse proceeding verse 11 that what is in question is EATING of blood and this is not pertaining to blood sacrifices.

Leviticus 17:10 *And whatsoever man there be of the house of Israel, or of the strangers that sojourn among them, that eateth any manner of blood, I will set My face against that soul that eateth blood, and will cut him off from among his people.*

Leviticus 17:11 *For the life of the flesh is in the blood; and I have given it to you upon the altar to make atonement for your souls; for it is the blood that maketh atonement by reason of the life.*

Leviticus 17:12 *Therefore I said unto the children of Israel: No soul of you shall eat blood, neither shall any stranger that sojourneth among you eat blood.*

However the verse does say that blood is "given to you upon the altar to make atonement for your souls." This verse does not say that blood is the only means for atonement. It basically says don't eat blood because it is used in sacrifices. But so too was incenses (Numbers 17:11-12) and golden ornaments (Numbers 31:50). The claim that blood is the only means of atonement is erroneous. In addition, blood sacrifices were mainly used for mistakes or transgressions done unintentionally (Leviticus 4:2, 13, 22, 27; 5:5, 15 and Numbers 15:27-31).

Also if a thief is caught and he lies in order to get out of the difficulty, he must sacrifice a ram (Lev. 5:24-26). These sacrifices of animals were the person's own property, not God's, as a symbol of the offender's sacrifice. And even as a literalist, Leviticus 17:11 says the blood of the sacrifice must be put on an altar to make atonement for sins, yet there is absolutely no passage of the Bible in which Jesus' (pbuh) blood was placed on an altar. Actually, death by crucifixion is due to asphyxiation or shock, not blood loss, which would disqualify Jesus (pbuh) from being a blood sacrifice as well. In fact, a blood atonement offering must be without blemish, scab, scar or injury (Lev 22:18-25). Due to the scourging of Jesus (pbuh) and the nails in his hands and feet, he is again disqualified from being a blood sacrifice.

According to the Old Testament, if anyone is a ransom for another, "The wicked is a ransom for the righteous" (Proverbs 21:18). It is the sin of the wicked that makes him a ransom, not the righteousness of an innocent man. Here again it is clear that the Old Testament does not substantiate the Christians' doctrine of atonement.

Yom Kippur

In preparation for Yom Kippur or the Day of Atonement, the law in Leviticus 16 describes the method used to make a grand atonement to God using an animal sacrifice. High priests, following the footsteps of

Aaron (pbuh), were commanded to sacrifice a ram and a goat for the atonement of "all their sins." But in order to complete this method, they must also "confess over him all the iniquities of the children of Israel, and all their transgressions, even all their sins; and he shall put them upon the head of the goat (another goat), and shall send him away by the hand of an appointed man into the wilderness." From this practice of placing all the blame and burden on this goat, we get the term scapegoat, because this goat ESCAPED DEATH. Therefore atonement for ALL SINS is acquired in the Old Testament with AND without sacrifice. And probably the most crucial point to be made here is that God made sacrifices obsolete in the Old Testament.

Hosea 14:2-3 *"Take words with you, And return to the LORD. Say to Him, "Take away all iniquity; receive us graciously, For we will render for bulls the offering of our lips."*

Hosea 6:6 *For I desire mercy, and not sacrifice, and the knowledge of G-d rather than burnt-offerings.*

Micah 6:6 *'Wherewith shall I come before HaShem, and bow myself before G-d on high? Shall I come before Him with burnt offerings, with calves of a year old?*

Micah 6:7 *Will HaShem be pleased with thousands of rams, with ten thousands of rivers of oil? Shall I give my first-born for my transgression, the fruit of my body for the sin of my soul?'*

Micah 6:8 *It hath been told thee, O man, what is good, and what HaShem doth require of thee: only to do justly, and to love mercy, and to walk humbly with thy G-d.*

Isaiah 1:11 *To what purpose is the multitude of your sacrifices unto Me? saith HaShem; I am full of the burnt-offerings of rams, and the fat of fed beasts; and I delight not in the blood of bullocks, or of lambs, or of he-goats.*

Isaiah 1:12 When ye come to appear before Me, who hath required this at your hand, to trample My courts?

Isaiah1:13 Bring no more vain oblations; it is an offering of abomination unto Me; new moon and Sabbath, the holding of convocations-- I cannot endure iniquity along with the solemn assembly.

Isaiah 1:14 Your new moons and your appointed seasons My soul hateth; they are a burden unto Me; I am weary to bear them.

Isaiah 1:15 And when ye spread forth your hands, I will hide Mine eyes from you; yea, when ye make many prayers, I will not hear; your hands are full of blood.

Isaiah 1:16 Wash you, make you clean, put away the evil of your doings from before Mine eyes, cease to do evil;

Isaiah 1:17 Learn to do well; seek justice, relieves the oppressed, judge the fatherless, plead for the widow.

Isaiah 43:25 I, even I, am He that blotteth out thy transgressions for Mine own sake; and thy sins I will not remember.

Isaiah 55:7 Let the wicked forsake his way, and the man of iniquity his thoughts; and let him return unto HaShem, and He will have compassion upon him, and to our G-d, for He will abundantly pardon

Proverbs 21:3 To do righteousness and justice is more acceptable to HaShem than sacrifice.

Psalms 51:17 O L-rd, open Thou my lips; and my mouth shall declare Thy praise.

Psalms 51:18 For Thou delightest not in sacrifice, else would I give it; Thou hast no pleasure in burnt-offering.

Psalms 40:6 Sacrifice and offering thou didst not desire; mine ears hast thou opened: burnt offering and sin offering hast thou not required.

HUMAN SACRIFICE

There is no Law of Moses (pbuh) which stipulates that a human being can be sacrificed for the atonement of another person's iniquities. In the Old Testament, there are cases of people attempting human sacrifice, but on each occasion, God intervenes and puts a halt to this action. In fact the laws of the Jewish Torah forbid human sacrifice as it was a practice done by polytheists.

Deuteronomy 12:30 *take heed to thyself that thou be not ensnared to follow them, after that they are destroyed from before thee; and that thou inquire not after their gods, saying: 'How used these nations to serve their gods? even so will I do likewise.'*

Deuteronomy 12:31 *Thou shalt not do so unto HaShem thy G-d; for every abomination to HaShem, which He hateth, have they done unto their gods; for even their sons and their daughters do they burn in the fire to their gods.*

It has been my experience that many Christians use the story of Abraham's (pbuh) sacrifice of his son as somewhat of a prophecy of God sending Jesus (pbuh), who is believed to be God's son, to be sacrificed. The glaring contradiction between the two stories is that the death of Abraham's (pbuh) son was not to be atonement for sin, but an affirmation of Abraham (pbuh) and his son's faith in God. Most importantly, Abraham's (pbuh) son was never killed.

God sent an angel to save his son before he was killed. Strangely enough, God sent an angel to Jesus (pbuh), as well, to STRENGTHEN him in his time of great need according to the gospels, but this is a point to be discussed later in this book. After the angel saved his son, Abraham (pbuh) gave a ram as a burnt offering to God instead of his son (Gen. 22:13). This offering was in the same vein as the offerings given to God by Cain and Abel. They were not for atonement of sin, but a testament of their devotion to God.

Most Biblical scholars view the story of Abraham (pbuh) and his son as a scene orchestrated by God to denounce the practice of human sacrifice, but many people have gotten the exact opposite impression. This is probably because the book of Hebrews portrays Abraham's (pbuh) story as a parallel to Jesus' (pbuh) last days.

Hebrews 11:17 By faith Abraham, when he was tried, offered up Isaac: and he that had received the promises offered up his only begotten [son],

Hebrews 11:18 Of whom it was said, That in Isaac shall thy seed be called:

Hebrews 11:19 Accounting that God [was] able to raise [him] up, even from the dead; from whence also he received him in a figure.

Though Isaac is not Abraham's (pbuh) only begotten son (Ishmael was), he is identified as such, but he is also said to have been raised from the dead, when it is well established and universally accepted that Isaac (pbuh) was never killed in this sacrifice. Thus the story of the sacrifice of Abraham serves the agenda of those who reject the crucifixion of Jesus (pbut) and it discredits the understanding of those who are proponents of Jesus' (pbuh) death on the cross. This is clear evidence that the Bible attests to someone being killed when they most definitely were not.

Moses (pbuh), perhaps the greatest prophet of the Hebrew Scriptures, attempted to sacrifice himself for the sins of the Israelites in the book of

Exodus. The children of Israel had broken the first and most important commandment of God, not to make any graven images of God and worship them besides God. This is the popular story of the Israelites making a golden calf to worship. This sin caused God great anger in the Jewish Torah. Moses (pbuh), because of his affinity for his people, sought to reconcile the relationship between the Israelites and God. Moses (pbuh) explicitly said that he would "make atonement for their sins" (Ex. 32:30). He returned to God and he asked God to either forgive the people or "blot him out of Thy book which Thou has written."

Moses (pbuh) was suggesting that God forget about him and wipe him and the memory of him off of the earth. The book Moses (pbuh) was referring to is God's figurative book of life of all his creations and creatures and their actions. Moses (pbuh) asked to have his life's achievements, including his family and his triumphs with the pharaoh for his people's freedom, expunged from history. If God accepted human sacrifices, we would have never heard of a mighty prophet named Moses (pbuh), but how did God respond to this human sacrifice?

Exodus 32:33 *And HaShem said unto Moses: 'Whosoever hath sinned against Me, him will I blot out of My book.*

Do not these words stand in direct opposition to the Christian idea of sin and forgiveness? God does not substitute the innocent in place of the guilty. Moses (pbuh) had done nothing wrong. He does not deserve punishment. And even if he desired to accept the penalty, God would not allow such an injustice. Some may object to the parallels that I have drawn by claiming that these individuals, Abraham's (pbuh) son and Moses (pbuh), were not qualified to be sacrifices for others' sin because they had committed sins themselves, whereas Jesus (pbuh) was totally sinless. It is true that the New Testament says that Jesus (pbuh) was sinless (2Cor. 5:21), but does the life of Jesus (pbuh) in the gospels

21

attest to this? This is a topic soon to be addressed.

Nonetheless, it is clear that there is absolutely no support for human sacrifice in the laws of Moses (pbuh) and there are examples to the contrary of such an idea. Also, sincere repentance actually did away with any sacrifice. Blood sacrifices, like the incenses and ornaments, were not the central point for forgiveness. The common theme throughout the Old Testament is repentance and a return to the right path. Blood sacrifice was so insignificant that the Old Testament says God renounced it as unnecessary for atonement. Thus Christians must stand their ground without the Hebrew Scriptures for support as it pertains to the Original Sin and their understanding of atonement for sin.

One of my favorite chapters in the Bible contains a verse very often used to bolster the Christian's view of sin and atonement. This verse must be used without its context because when put into context, it rips to shreds the Christians' doctrine of inherited sin, blood sacrifices, the belief that someone else will carry your burden for you and the belief that man is incapable of salvation without an intercessor between him and God.

__Ezekiel 18:20__ The soul that sinneth, it shall die; the son shall not bear the iniquity of the father with him, neither shall the father bear the iniquity of the son with him; the righteousness of the righteous shall be upon him, and the wickedness of the wicked shall be upon him.

__Ezekiel 18:21__ But if the wicked turn from all his sins that he hath committed, and keep all My statutes, and do that which is lawful and right, he shall surely live, he shall not die.

__Ezekiel 18:22__ None of his transgressions that he hath committed shall be remembered against him; for his righteousness that he hath done he shall live.

The words "live" and "die" are not used literally in this instance. They pertain to the hereafter. To live means to dwell in the kingdom of Heaven. To die is to live in hell. So we can see that you gain salvation by living righteously. And if you sin, you must repent and turn from your sinful ways and you will gain salvation in heaven. When these verses are juxtaposed the doctrine of Christianity it is, without doubt, proof that two contradicting doctrines exist in the Bible and they cannot be adhere to simultaneously. You cannot believe that sin is inherited and it is not inherited. You cannot believe that someone else bears your sin and that you bear your own sins. You cannot believe that it is impossible to gain entrance into heaven on your own and believe that it is possible to enter heaven on your own. One must chose, which is the more rational, more logical, more righteous, more responsible and the more godly approach.

PUT THE FOCUS ON JESUS (pbuh)

Since the idea of Original Sin and atonement are not based in the Old Testament, it is of little use for Christians to maintain that the Old Testament is in support of these doctrines. Their existence and support are from the New Testament. And the 27 books of the New Testament have one focal point, Jesus Christ (pbuh). Though 23 of the 27 books are visions, ideas and dreams about Jesus (pbuh), four of the books are what is reported to be his actual words and actions on earth. I intend to show that just as these doctrines are not present in the Old Testament, they are nonexistent in the teaching of Jesus (pbuh), as well. This leaves their origin in the minds of those who wrote about Jesus (pbuh), only.

My focal point now will be on what was Jesus' (pbuh) message, to whom was his message geared, was Jesus (pbuh) worthy to be a sacrifice for mankind (was he sinless?) and finally I will scrutinize the accounts of his crucifixion. In order to clarify Jesus' (pbuh) teaching, I will use each gospel record individually to pinpoint what each author's perspective of Jesus' (pbuh) mission was. And because the gospels are not identical stories, but each contains aspects of Jesus' (pbuh) life exclusively found in their respective biography, I will piece together these points of Jesus (pbuh) supposed crucifixion where possible.

CHAPTER III – THE GOSPEL OF MATTHEW

The book of Matthew is believed to be the second gospel written. It is commonly attributed to a former tax collector and disciple of Jesus (pbuh), called Matthew or Levi. The audience his book is addressing is Jews. His aim is to present Jesus (pbuh) as the fulfillment of the Old Testament's prophecies of the Messiah.

Matthew's book is filled with quotations from the Old Testament which he says foretold the life of Jesus Christ (pbuh). Matthew is probably the most explicit when it comes to defining Jesus' (pbuh) targeted audience.

JESUS' (pbuh) MESSAGE IN GOSPEL OF MATTHEW

Follow the Laws

According to the book believed to be written by a disciple of Jesus (pbuh), Matthew, Jesus' (pbuh) message was not this human sacrifice for the forgiveness of sins, but self-accountability for one's own sins. In other words, Jesus' (pbuh) message for salvation was in total agreement with the prevailing message of atonement for sin found in the Old Testament. It is true that Jesus (pbuh) was said to save "his people" from their sins (1:21) but the question is, how was he to do this? First off, Jesus (pbuh) made it crystal clear in the book of Matthew that his goal was to "keep the laws of Moses (pbuh)."

__5:17__ Think not that I am come to destroy the law, or the prophets: I am not come to destroy, but to fulfill.

__5:18__ For verily I say unto you, Till heaven and earth pass, one jot or one tittle shall in no wise pass from the law, till all be fulfilled.

__5:19__ Whosoever therefore shall break one of these least commandments, and shall teach men so, he shall be called the least in the kingdom of heaven: but whosoever shall do and teach them, the same shall be called great in the kingdom of heaven.

It is critical to understand that Jesus (pbuh) commands his followers to keep the laws of the Old Testament down to the smallest letter, "jot" or "tittle." And those who follow and teach the law will be called great and those who do not follow or teach the laws will be called "the least." I want you to consider, how the laws of Moses (pbuh) have become obsolete in almost all circles of Christianity? How is it that his disciples have dreams or visions and Christians are now able to "break one of these least commandments"? This is solely because they have taken the words of disciples and leaders over the words of Jesus (pbuh). This has resulted in a totally different system of religion than the one taught by Jesus (pbuh).

Paul says the law is nailed to the cross (Col. 2:14). Jesus (pbuh) says the law will last until heaven and earth pass away. Who are you to believe, Jesus (pbuh) or Paul? According to the words of Jesus (pbuh), Paul and Peter and anyone else who teaches against the laws are called "the least" in the kingdom of heaven. Yet these two men are given honor and recognition in the Bible for their books of authority. This authority is over their very own master's words. Also, it is to be understood that when Jesus (pbuh) says they will be called the least in the kingdom of heaven, he means they will be called the least by God or his heavenly hosts. It does not mean that the offenders of the law will enter heaven and then be called the least, because we will soon see that you can't get into heaven without following the laws.

And Jesus (pbuh) said he came to "fulfill" the laws which by definition mean to carry through, or to put in effect. Many misconstrue the word "fulfill" to mean that Jesus (pbuh) will satisfy the laws through his death. Some people have preconceived notions and they insert them into Jesus' (pbuh) teachings. For example, if you are already under the impression that Jesus' sole purpose was to die for the sins of the world and the law is nailed to the cross, you will understand "all is fulfilled" to mean because he died, you no longer have to obey the laws. However, to those who read the book of Matthew in its context, it is easy to understand that by fulfill, it means "to put in effect" and follow the laws of Moses (pbuh), as Jesus (pbuh) himself did. This idea of his death as an adherence to the entire law is actually the demise of the law, which he specifically said was not his mission. And Jesus (pbuh) elaborates further on what his followers must do to attain heaven.

Jesus (pbuh) said if your righteous actions do not exceed the scribes' and Pharisees' RIGHTEOUSNESS, then you WILL NOT ENTER THE KINGDOM OF HEAVEN (5:20). Perhaps as a warning to those who are to follow him, Jesus (pbuh) said that everyone who speaks in his name will not enter heaven, only the person "that doeth the will of my Father which is in heaven" (7:21). What is the will of the Father? His will for man is in the law. Jesus (pbuh) gave the formula to get to heaven. FOLLOW THE LAWS! Yet his words are void of any reference to his death. And just to solidify this point, I will give an example.

A man came to Jesus and plainly asked him, "What must I do to gain eternal life." And Jesus (pbuh) told him to KEEP THE COMMANDMENTS. The man said, "I have kept these commandments since I was a child." Jesus (pbuh) responded, if you want to be PERFECT sell you possessions, give the money to the poor and follow me. However the man declined because he loved his worth too dearly (19:16-24). This is an excellent illustration of Jesus' (pbuh) message to his disciples. Jesus (pbuh) clearly said that you get to heaven by following the laws. Was Jesus (pbuh) lying when he said this? Why did he not say, I come to take on the sin of the world, believe in my death which will occur in a couple of years and you will automatically be put on the road to heaven? Because this is not what Jesus (pbuh) taught as the way to heaven. His teachings were to follow the laws and if you already followed the laws, exceed your own righteousness.

When Jesus (pbuh) says to become "perfect," he is implying that the man is righteous but that he must move to the next level, yet the man was unwilling to do so. Just as Jesus (pbuh) told this man to follow him, Jesus (pbuh) told others to do the same. This was one of Jesus' (pbuh) coined phrases, "take your cross and follow me" (16:24). He did not mean to get crucified, but Jesus (pbuh) wanted them to carry their responsibilities, the way that he carries his. He is asking his followers to detach themselves from that which they longed for in this world in order to follow his words and actions (5:29-30). And Jesus (pbuh) followed the laws of Moses (pbuh). In order to be Christ-like, Christians must do the same.

The scribes and Pharisees were already following the laws, just like the rich man. And Jesus (pbuh) says be more righteous than they. Righteous means characterized by or proceeding from accepted standards of morality or justice. The standards of morality and justice are given in the law. You can't exceed righteousness by not keeping laws, but simply believing in a particular event. So by definition, you must follow all the laws and more in order to enter heaven according to Jesus (pbuh). So how is exceeding the righteousness of the scribes and Pharisees accomplished.

23:1 *Then Jesus said to the crowds and to his disciples:*

23:2 *"The teachers of the law and the Pharisees sit in Moses' seat."*

23: 3 *So you must obey them and do everything they tell you. But do not do what they do, for they do not practice what they preach.*

So in order to be more righteous than someone else, you must outdo them in the laws and in good deeds and abstain from even more evil actions than they. And Jesus (pbuh) does not leave this to our imagination. Jesus (pbuh) administered revisions to the laws, which he began to articulate immediately after declaring that their righteousness must be exceeded. What Jesus (pbuh) does is he began to abrogate laws of Moses (pbuh). He loosens some restrictions and he tightens others. He was curing the ailments of the Jews, which they garnered due to strict adherence without considering the spirit and principle of the law.

Many of Moses' (pbuh) laws were for his time period. The Jews were a nomadic people. They had no time for lengthy trials. So their justice was swift and straightforward, i.e. "an eye for an eye." Inevitably the Jews lost compassion and a sense of justice and they began to administer punishment without consideration for the cause for the crime. Jesus (pbuh) sought to rectify this problem, thus his amendment was to "turn the other cheek." In the case of divorce, these nomadic Jews had no time for divorce court, so divorce was made easy in the laws of Moses (pbuh). This apparently was abused. In order to stop this abuse, Jesus (pbuh) restricted the divorce laws (Matt. 5:31-32). And he reiterated that man is not to commit adultery. But to exceed the level of righteousness of the scribes and Pharisees, now Jesus (pbuh) said don't even look upon a woman to lust after her (Matt. 5:28). On the more spiritual note, when the Jews fasted they made it a public spectacle, thus Jesus (pbuh) said when you fast, it is between you and God and you should carry on as if you are not fasting (Matt. 6:16-18). In any case, it is obvious that Jesus (pbuh) is giving his followers the path to exceeding the righteousness of the scribes and Pharisees with no mention of his death as a requirement for heaven. This is a glimpse of Jesus' (pbuh) teaching:

10:34 *Think not that I am come to send peace on earth: I came not to send peace, but a sword.*

10:35 *For I am come to set a man at variance against his father, and the daughter against her mother, and the daughter in law against her mother in law.*

10:36 *And a man's foes shall be they of his own household.*

10:37 *He that loveth father or mother more than me is not worthy of me: and he that loveth son or daughter more than me is not worthy of me.*

10:38 *And he that taketh not his cross, and followeth after me, is not worthy of me.*

The words "I am come to" throughout the gospels should be of great significance to a Christian and anyone seeking the truth of Jesus' (pbuh) message because he is spelling out his purpose on earth. His purpose is to have a person forsake anything that is not in adherence to his teachings. When he speaks of love in these verses, it is actually obedience which he is stressing, not emotional feelings. He is saying that you are to obey my rules even if they conflict with what your family wishes for you. That is why he ends with "take up your cross and follow me." He means that you should carry your responsibility and burden as he carries his. Jesus (pbuh) is setting the example by which you must follow despite anything else. And this is the method that every prophet uses. Jesus (pbuh) is ordering his followers, not simply to believe, but to "do," to do as he does, to pray as he prays, to fast as he fasts, to act as he acts, to forgive as he does.

Forgiveness

In the very same breath that Jesus (pbuh) abrogated the laws for the Jews, he also taught his followers how to pray to God. In this prayer is Jesus' (pbuh) understanding of forgiveness, which is very significant in understanding the proper view of atonement for sins, as well as man's inclination to sin.

6:12 *And forgive us our debts, as we forgive our debtors.*

6:13 *And lead us not into temptation, but deliver us from evil: For thine is the kingdom, and the power, and the glory, forever.*

6:14 *For if ye forgive men their trespasses, your heavenly Father will also forgive you:*

6:15 *But if ye forgive not men their trespasses, neither will your Father forgive your trespasses. Amen.*

We can deduce from these words that Jesus (pbuh) taught that man must seek God's guidance and power to avoid sin. Therefore with God's help and his own determination, man can achieve his own salvation without an innocent person's sacrifice. Even though, God aid's man in his salvation, it is man's initiative to be righteous that God seeks, thus he is not hopelessly a sinner (as many Christians suggest). In fact, I would say that human beings are more righteous by nature than sinful. Most people are good, not evil. Simply because you sin and because many believe all sins to be equal, people are called sinners. Yet they are reluctant to call people righteous, when the person performs righteous deeds, because he may have done something sinful in his life. This is purely a human concept, that one sin makes you a sinner. If this is the case then one good deed makes you righteous. (Luckily, God knows and judges ALL our deeds, the good and the bad, and which ever outweighs the other, is how he discerns whether we are righteous or wicked).

Nonetheless, Jesus (pbuh) also describes forgiveness and its workings. It appears to me that one can achieve forgiveness by showing mercy and forgiveness to others or by asking for forgiveness for themselves. And how does Jesus (pbuh) say forgiveness eludes you? First, what might a Christians say in response to this question? He probably would say you are not forgiven unless you believe in the blood of Jesus Christ (pbuh), as Paul said (Romans 5:8-9). But Jesus (pbuh) said you will not receive forgiveness, if you do not forgive others. Jesus (pbuh) even gave a parable in which he illustrates that God's forgiveness is based upon your treatment of others (18:23-35). Who must you follow, Jesus (pbuh) or Paul?

Repentance

Jesus (pbuh) said that his followers will be rewarded for their works (16:27) and that faith and deeds are intertwined (17:20-21). Jesus (pbuh) is not speaking of faith in his death, because he had not died yet, but faith in his words and God's will. But if one were to sin, he must be forgiving to others and be repentant. Once again Jesus (pbuh) gives another decree of his purpose on earth.

9:12 On hearing this, Jesus said, "It is not the healthy who need a doctor, but the sick.

9:13 But go and learn what this means: 'I desire mercy, not sacrifice.' For I have not come to call the righteous, but sinners."

We notice that Jesus (pbuh), as a spokesmen for God, says he doesn't want sacrifice. This is plain and straightforward. God wants his servants to show mercy to one another. This far exceeds any sacrifice that they may make to him. Also in this verse, Jesus (pbuh) declares that his duty is to call sinners to repent. He is only here for those who need assistance. You see, the Pharisees were upset with Jesus (pbuh) because he was entertaining sinners. But Jesus (pbuh) says he came for the sinners, not the righteous. Thus Jesus (pbuh) did not come for all people, according to his own words.

FOR WHOM WAS JESUS' (pbuh) MESSAGE INTENDED?

Universal Laws?

If we analyze the laws that Jesus (pbuh) abrogated, we find that much of Jesus' (pbuh) teaches are time bound and set for specific conditions. Is it practical to allow remarriage only if someone has commit adultery in the relationship (19:9)? Divorce should be the last resort and done after all other avenues are exhausted, but there are circumstances, besides infidelity, in which divorce is more beneficial to both parties involved. What if a spouse is abusive mentally or physically with the other spouse or the children? Is this not acceptable ground for divorce? Yet Jesus (pbuh) doesn't allow for divorce and remarriage in this situation. If you were to remarry, you have committed adultery in Jesus' (pbuh) eyes.

Other laws which are impractical in usage outside of specific circumstances are to "turn the other cheek", "if you are sued for your coat, give him your cloak as well" and "give whatever anyone asks of you." I would love to learn of any country willing to implement these rules into practice or even a person who wishes to live by this code of ethics. It is extraordinary when someone implores one of these methods, but it is impossible to live in peace if one were to implore them all. I wish to meet the Christian who will reject self-defense, quietly allow someone to relieve him of his possessions, and give them anything else that he asks for. As Ahmed Deedat once said, you would be "encouraging the bully to give you a beating. Who would say, when they found someone interfering with his sister, 'Hey I have another sister at home!!'"

Because Jesus' (pbuh) laws are not suitable for all of mankind, this gives rise to the question, "who was Jesus' (pbuh) message for?"

Is it Few or Many?

The author of the Book of Matthew is confused as to how many people were to receive and accept the message of Jesus (pbuh).

few there be that find it (the straight path) (7:14).

for many be called, but few chosen (20:16).

For many are called, but few are chosen (22:14).

And I say unto you, That many shall come ... in the kingdom of heaven (8:11).

For this is my blood of the new testament, which is shed for many for the remission of sins (26:28).

These quotations may cause some readers to assume that Jesus (pbuh) is the person who is confused about his number of followers. Of course, few and many mean different things to different people, but all of these words are supposed to be spoken by one person, Jesus (pbuh). Is it a coincidence that he does not say "all" in any of these quotations? If he were to be a savior for the world, shouldn't he have said "all are called, but few are chosen" or "my blood is shed for all for remission of sin." And Jesus (pbuh) gave the reason why all people will not get his message. It is because some people are not worthy of his message and blessings at all.

_7:6_ *Give not that which is holy unto the dogs, neither cast ye your pearls before swine, lest they trample them under their feet, and turn again and rend you*

Jesus (pbuh) gave his disciples the power to heal sickness and disease and to cast out devils. His disciples, who were all Jews, were specifically told NOT to preach or heal the gentiles or non-Jew.

_10:6_ *But go rather to the lost sheep of the house of Israel.*

If your mission is for the whole of mankind, why would you start off by excluding the majority of humanity from your preaching and healing? Jesus (pbuh) purposely ignored the problems of the non- Jews. He told his disciples not to even go in the direction or "way" of the gentiles nor to "enter the city of the Samaritans." And Jesus (pbuh) narrows down his following even further.

He is only interested in "the lost sheep," which implies that a percentage of the house of Israel was in no need of salvation. If you are not lost, then you must be on the right path or you are at your destination already. The problem is that Jesus (pbuh) was not even close to being crucified when he gave this command to his disciples. So Jesus (pbuh) sent his disciples to only a specific group of the Israelites, the lost sheep, but to whom was Jesus (pbuh) sent?

We do not have to read pass the first chapter of Matthew to find out that Jesus has come to "save HIS PEOPLE from their sins (Matthew 1:21). Who are Jesus' (pbuh) people? Jesus (pbuh) was born in the lineage of the Israelites which Matthew acknowledges in the first chapter. Therefore his people are the Children of Israel.

This statement alone by Matthew contradicts any other statement attributing Jesus' (pbuh) mission to ANYONE other than the children of Israel. This proclamation is from the angel of the Lord to Mary. He gave her the news of a son named Jesus (pbuh), who will save "his people" from their sins. The angel told Mary Jesus' (pbuh) agenda in a nutshell. If Jesus (pbuh) was to save the world from sin, wouldn't it be more appropriate to say so at that juncture. The difference between "his people" and the world is not something we can call insignificant.

The wise men come from the east to Jerusalem seeking the "King of the Jews" (2:1-2). This is in complete congruency with the proclamation made by the angel to Mary. Even more unambiguous is Jesus (pbuh) very own words about for whom his message is intended.

***15:24** But he answered and said, I am not sent but unto the lost sheep of the house of Israel.*

Can anyone be more explicit than this? The only way to clarify his position any further is to actually call the names of the people he came for. And we find in chapter 18 Jesus' (pbuh) explanation of who were the lost sheep of the house of Israel.

***18:11** For the Son of man is come to save that which was lost.*

***18:12** How think ye? if a man have an hundred sheep, and one of them be gone astray, doth he not leave the ninety and nine, and goeth into the mountains, and seeketh that which is gone astray?*

***18:13** And if so be that he find it, verily I say unto you, he rejoiceth more of that sheep, than of the ninety and nine which went not astray.*

***18:14** Even so it is not the will of your Father which is in heaven, that one of these little ones should perish.*

It is abundantly clear that Jesus (pbuh) was only here for the guidance of those specific Jews who had fallen off course on the road to heaven. If we are to take his words literally, he only came for one percent of the Jews. It has been the prerogative of some Christians to maintain that Jesus (pbuh) came for the Jews first, then the non-Jews. However Jesus' (pbuh) explanation of the lost Jews nullifies this argument, because he didn't even come for all the Jews and he ignored the gentiles and made his disciples to do so, as well. Not to mention, if Jesus (pbuh) were sent to the Jews, and then the world, it would mean that he was either misinformed or misinforming others when he said "I am NOT sent "BUT" unto the lost sheep of the house of Israel." That means he was ONLY sent to them. Had Jesus (pbuh) been sent to the world, he would not have said "not" and "but." He would have said I am sent to them, "first", then the world.

Another explanation given by Christians to signify that Jesus (pbuh) came for the entire world is the context of the story when Jesus (pbuh) says that he only came for the lost sheep. There was a Canaanite woman, a non-Jew, who had a daughter possessed by the devil. She came to Jesus (pbuh), so he could heal her daughter. At which point Jesus (pbuh) totally ignores the woman and her request.

_15:23_ _But he answered her not a word._

The disciples told Jesus (pbuh) to "send her away," at which point Jesus (pbuh) said to his disciples, "I am not sent but unto the lost sheep of the house of Israel." But the woman is persistent. She begs more earnestly for Jesus (pbuh) to help her. Jesus (pbuh) says his blessing are for the children, the lost sheep, and that she is not worthy of receiving those blessings. This Canaanite woman will not take no for an answer. She accepts Jesus' (pbuh) belittlement and she asks for a bit of the lost sheep's blessing. And Jesus (pbuh) grants this to her for her persistent and faith in him and he heals her daughter.

Once again, the Christian is forced to conclude that the ends justify the means. They deduce that Jesus (pbuh) did heal the gentile child, so Jesus (pbuh) did come for the non-Jews. Well why did Jesus (pbuh) not make others go through such an ordeal and bearing of insults in order for him to heal them of their sickness or disease? The answer is in Jesus' (pbuh) own words.

_7:6_ _Give not that which is holy unto the dogs, neither cast ye your pearls before swine, lest they trample them under their feet, and turn again_ *and rend you.*

7:7 *Ask, and it shall be given you; seek, and ye shall find; knock, and it shall be opened unto you:*

7:8 *For every one that asketh receiveth; and he that seeketh findeth; and to him that knocketh it shall be opened*

Jesus (pbuh), when first approached by the woman, ignored her, as he had his disciple do to all gentiles. When the disciples asked him to send her away and the woman worshipped him, he said, as he told his disciples earlier, that his blessing are for "the lost sheep." Was he lying to the disciples and this woman? No, he is placing this gentile woman as one amongst the dogs and swine who is not worthy or appreciative of his blessings. However, the woman continued to beg and as verses 7 and 8 of chapter 7 indicate, even if an unworthy person asks, the thing will be given to them. Therefore the fact that Jesus (pbuh) healed the Canaanite child does not indicate that he was sent to them, but that he was obligated to heal her if her mother persisted. The children of Israel did not have to succumb to such indignation in order to receive their blessings, because the blessing was theirs to begin with. Time and time again, Jesus (pbuh) healed people without slandering them. Why does he make an exception in this case? Because according to the Gospel of Matthew, he was giving the children's blessing to someone undeserving.

We must bear in mind that there are often two opposing views in the Bible and this topic is no exception. I have conclusively given Jesus' (pbuh) position on who was to receive his message from his own words. But there are ample verses which stipulate that Jesus (pbuh) was sent to the Jews and non-Jews. Matthew's book is filled with references to the Old Testament's prophecies. One prophecy of Isaiah which Matthew cites was that Jesus (pbuh) will show the gentiles judgment and they will trust in his name (12:17-21). The problem is that the prophecy also states that this person in the prophecy will not strive, cry or have his voice heard in the streets, when, in fact, Jesus (pbuh) was guilty of all these things (Mark 9:19, Luke 19:41, Matt 23:1). Perhaps Matthew believed Jesus (pbuh) was to deliver his message to the gentiles as well, but the evidence he presents to verify this claims is erroneous and contrary to the words of Jesus (pbuh).

Another example is when Jesus (pbuh) is said to have told his disciples to teach the gospel to the entire world. The major problem is that this assignment was given in the midst of a false prophecy attributed to Jesus (pbuh). Jesus (pbuh) is said to have mentioned the details of the end of the world (24:5-36) and one of them is that Jesus' (pbuh) gospel will be preached to the world. But Jesus (pbuh) placed the end of the world DURING THE LIFETIME OF THE DISCIPLES (24:22-24). I am baffled as to how his message would reach the entire world in such a short time without fax machines, phones, internet, planes and an abundance of literate people. Perhaps Jesus (pbuh) or whoever spoke this prophecy had a different meaning for the "world" than what is commonly understood today. (We shall soon see.) At any rate, it is apparent that the world did not end, thus the declaration that Jesus (pbuh) wanted the world to hear his message is to be taken with a grain of salt.

WAS JESUS (pbuh) WORTHY TO BE A SACRIFICE?

In order for Jesus (pbuh) to be a sacrifice for mankind, Jesus (pbuh) must be sinless. And according to Paul (2 Cor. 5:21), Peter (1Pet. 2:22) and Christianity, Jesus (pbuh) was sinless? But according to the gospel of Matthew, he was not. Jesus (pbuh) called people dogs and pigs (7:6).

Both animals are frown upon in comparison to humans, especially the pig, which is called unclean in the Law of Moses (pbuh) (Lev. 11:7-8). Jesus (pbuh) is constantly telling his followers to "take up the cross and follow him." In order to fully accomplish this, they must call others dogs and pigs, as well, but this is a clear insult. Yet Jesus (pbuh) speaks very disparagingly towards those who insult others. Matthew records Jesus (pbuh) as saying, if you call someone a fool, you will go to hell (5:22).

Apparently insulting people is a grave sin, but by this decree Jesus (pbuh) qualifies himself for hellfire when he twice called people "fools" (23:17, 19). How hypocritical Matthew portrays Jesus (pbuh) to be. He ordains hell for anyone to say this, but he does it himself. If it is a sin for me to do, is it not a sin for Jesus (pbuh)?

Some people rationalize that he has authority to say these things. If this is the case, then he is not really sinless or his sinlessness is not as impressive as advertised. The whole idea of his sinlessness was that he was tempted, just as every other man is tempted, throughout his life, yet he resisted evil and did not transgress the laws. But if he was given authority to break laws, even the ones he administered, then he is not really sinless, he is immune to the laws, which is a huge difference. Unfortunately, for those who hold this view, Jesus' (pbuh) words betray this argument, because he came to "fulfill the law."

Let's say, he was somehow justified in violating his own law about calling people fools, what about innocent people? Can he belittle them as well? One of his would-be disciples agreed to follow Jesus (pbuh), but only after he buried his dead father.

8:22 *But Jesus said unto him, Follow me; and let the dead bury their dead.*

In this instance, Jesus (pbuh) insulted all the people involved in burying this man. He insulted his disciple's mother and any other of their family and friends on their day of mourning. And by beckoning this disciple to abandon his father, he insulted his father as not being important enough to be buried by this disciple. I guess this kind of attitude should not come as a surprise considering how Jesus (pbuh) spoke of this own family.

It would seem that Jesus (pbuh) held all parents in high regard, considering that he felt to curse your mother or father is grounds for the death penalty (15:4). But his attitude towards his family seemed to contrast with this idea. One day, Jesus' (pbuh) mother and his brothers came looking for Jesus (pbuh) to speak with him. Jesus (pbuh) was informed of this, "But he answered and said unto him that told him, who is my mother? and who are my brethren? And he stretched forth his hand toward his disciples, and said, Behold my mother and my brethren! For whosoever shall do the will of my Father which is in heaven, the same is my brother, and sister, and mother" (12:48-50).

Jesus (pbuh), being an example for these disciples to follow, pitted himself against his own family as he said was his goal for all his disciples (10:35-37). If we are to believe the book of Matthew, Jesus (pbuh) denounced his blood family and claimed the disciples as his real family and he never responded to this family's request, at all. But these disciples, whom he considered his family, were not safe from Jesus' (pbuh) wrath either.

Jesus (pbuh) called them a "faithless and perverse generation" (17:17). In this case, it appears that Jesus (pbuh) was rebuking the disciples because they could not heal a sick boy, due to their lack of faith according to Jesus (17:19-20). If Jesus (pbuh) was not speaking to his disciples, the only alternative was that Jesus (pbuh) was speaking ill of the father and his sick son, which would not be the first time that Jesus (pbuh) insulted the hapless. If you recall the story of the Canaanite woman and her possessed daughter, you will remember that Jesus (pbuh) not only called the mother a dog but he also called the sick girl a dog, simply because she is not Jewish.

And finally, Jesus (pbuh) drank wine (11:19). Imbibing alcohol is a sin according to the Bible. I am aware, that there are verses in the Bible which permit alcohol, but there are also verses which prohibit it. Church leaders are prohibited from drinking wine (1Tim. 3:3). This is because drinking wine makes you weak (Romans 14:21). Great men of the Bible fell, one by one, due to alcohol consumption. David, Lot and Noah (phut), according to the Bible, all succumb to weakness and sin through alcohol. In light of this, people like the Nazirites were prohibited from drinking wine (Judges 13:7), and John the Baptist (pbuh) is praised for his abstinence (Luke 1:15). Yet we find that Jesus (pbuh) drank wine and his disciples drank wine even after Jesus (pbuh) left this earth (Acts 2:13-15). Had not Jesus (pbuh) read the book of Proverbs?

Proverbs 31:4 *It is not for kings, O Lemuel, it is not for kings to drink wine; nor for princes strong drink:*

Proverbs 31:5 *Lest they drink, and forget the law, and pervert the judgment of any of the afflicted.*

Some Christians believe drinking alcohol is permissible, but drunkenness is prohibited, but it is clear that those of power, lawmakers, church leaders, kings and prince are not to drink at all. Therefore, Jesus (pbuh) has transgressed the limits set by God, on more than one occasion. Thus he is not qualified to be a sacrifice for the sins of man. This means, even if he was crucified, its only result would be his death.

CHAPTER IV – THE GOSPEL OF MARK

The gospel according to Mark was written to the Romans and it is believed to be the first gospel written. It contains many similarities with the gospels according to Matthew and Luke. Because of these similarities, it is believed by most scholars that Matthew and Luke used Mark's book to formulate their own gospels. Along with similarities, there are also notable differences between these gospels. Some differences are in the sequence of events, some are in the number of participants in a certain event and other differences are in the words used by Jesus (pbuh) or those around him. It is possibly human error or an imperfect memory which accounts for these discrepancies. Some differences are quite insignificant, while others are of great importance when one is attempting to uncover the mission of Jesus (pbuh).

FOR WHOM WAS JESUS' (pbuh) MESSAGE INTENDED?

When I was searching for the audience in which Jesus (pbuh) was to deliver his message, I came across a story of Mark which seems quite similar to one in Matthew. There came a woman to Jesus (pbuh) with a daughter with an unclean spirit. The woman fell at Jesus (pbuh) feet and asked him to heal her daughter.

7:26 *The woman was a Greek, a Syrophenician by nation; and she besought him that he would cast forth the devil out of her daughter.*

7:27 *But Jesus said unto her, Let the children first be filled: for it is not meet to take the children's bread, and to cast it unto the dogs.*

7:28 *And she answered and said unto him, Yes, Lord: yet the dogs under the table eat of the children's crumbs.*

The story of Matthew maintains that this was a Canaanite woman and in it Jesus (pbuh) clearly stated that he only came for the lost sheep. Mark, on the other hand, does not contain the depiction of Jesus (pbuh) ignoring the woman or Jesus' (pbuh) reference to the lost sheep. What Mark does have is the Christian's bolster that Jesus (pbuh) came to give his blessings to the Jews FIRST. But Jesus (pbuh) did not explicitly say "after the Jews get their blessing, then non-Jews will get their fill," but it is implied.

However the woman said that she only required the leftover blessings and Jesus healed her daughter because of this response, which might also imply that non-Jews only get the scraps at the table, as Matthew's gospel suggests. And Jesus (pbuh) still called the non-Jews, dogs who are not worthy of the blessing that he provides. Though Mark's account of this story is a bit different and ambiguous, if read alongside the gospel of Matthew, it is apparent that the two agree that Jesus (pbuh) was to come to the Jews and the non-Jews were an afterthought. Is there a conflict amongst them about Jesus' (pbuh) message to his followers?

JESUS' (pbuh) MESSAGE IN THE GOSPEL OF MARK

Follow the Law

God plainly tells believers in Jesus (pbuh) to "hear him" (9:7), not to hear what everyone said about him. Jesus (pbuh) went out before a multitude of people and "taught them" (2:13, 6:6). He did not teach them the gospels of Matthew, Mark, Luke and John. Nor did he teach them the epistles of Paul. Though his final actions are held in high regard, it is HIS message which is of THE GREATEST importance. So what did he have to say?

7:6 He answered and said unto them, Well hath Esaias prophesied of you hypocrites, as it is written, This people honoureth me with their lips, but their heart is far from me.

7:7 Howbeit in vain do they worship me, teaching for doctrines the commandments of men.

7:8 For laying aside the commandment of God, ye hold the tradition of men, as the washing of pots and cups: and many other such like things ye do.

__7:9__ And he said unto them, Full well ye reject the commandment of God, that ye may keep your own tradition.

In these words, we find confirmation that Jesus (pbuh) ordered his followers to obey the laws of Moses (pbuh), which gives the rules of atonement for sins. Human sacrifice for sins is nowhere to be found in the commandments, therefore it is a "tradition of men" which Christians adhere to, while "laying aside the commandments of God." The premise that the law is to be adhered to is also illustrated in a conversation between Jesus (pbuh) and a scribe.

__12:28__ And one of the scribes came, and having heard them reasoning together, and perceiving that he had answered them well, asked him, Which is the first commandment of all?

__12:29__ And Jesus answered him, The first of all the commandments is, Hear, O Israel; The Lord our God is one Lord:

__12:30__ And thou shalt love the Lord thy God with all thy heart, and with all thy soul, and with all thy mind, and with all thy strength: this is the first commandment.

__12:31__ And the second is like, namely this, Thou shalt love thy neighbour as thyself. There is none other commandment greater than these.

__12:32__ And the scribe said unto him, Well, Master, thou hast said the truth: for there is one God; and there is none other but he:

__12:33__ And to love him with all the heart, and with all the understanding, and with all the soul, and with all the strength, and to love his neighbour as himself, is more than all whole burnt offerings and sacrifices.

__12:34__ And when Jesus saw that he answered discreetly, he said unto him, Thou art not far from the kingdom of God. And no man after that *durst ask him any question.*

Jesus (pbuh) assured this man that he is on the path to heaven, by simply following the commandments of God. Was Jesus (pbuh) pulling his leg? Did Jesus (pbuh) forget to tell him, that it is incumbent of this scribe to believe in Jesus' (pbuh) demise? Was it not incumbent on Jesus (pbuh) to explain that his death is what must be believed in, in order to achieve this final goal? The problem is that Jesus (pbuh) never, ever said this, in his life, as his last words or during his supposed resurrection. The reason for this omission is simple. Belief in his death was not a part of his message and it was not necessary to believe in it to be saved. The scribe who follows all the laws of God, is he less righteous or less godly if he does not believe Jesus' (pbuh) death was for his sins and his only way to heaven? Of course not, especially considering that Jesus (pbuh) told him he was already on his way to heaven.

Repentance

We find that John the Baptist (pbuh) taught the baptism of repentance for the forgiveness of sins and John (pbuh) had a huge following. He baptizes ALL of Judea and Jerusalem (1:4-5). And all of John the Baptist's (pbuh) follower went to Jesus. John (pbuh) had already prepped them for Jesus' (pbuh) teachings of forgiveness of sins. John (pbuh) said "I baptize with water, but he (Jesus) baptizes with the Holy Spirit (1:8). Whatever one may consider the Holy Spirit to be, it is apparent that this baptism is to be given while Jesus (pbuh) was alive to his followers, which means they had sins forgiven though Jesus (pbuh) without his death. And as John (pbuh) did, Jesus (pbuh) preached repentance (2:17) and he commanded his disciples to teach repentance (6:12). When those who heard this message repented, were they forgiven or not?

Forgiveness

In Mark, Jesus (pbuh) taught that forgiveness is granted to the sinner making an effort towards God as God bestowing his mercy on the person. A sacrifice is not needed. Loving God and loving your neighbors is better than ALL sacrifices (12:33). Forgiveness is granted to those who forgive others (11:25-26). Anytime a person is converted to the belief in Jesus (pbuh), all his sins are forgiven (4:12). And Jesus (pbuh) according to Mark was given the authority to forgive sins.

Jesus (pbuh) implies that it is easier for him to forgive sins than to heal a sick man, yet he does both (2:5-12). If Jesus (pbuh) can easily forgive sins based upon sheer faith of a person, doesn't it stand to reason that God has even less difficulty? He is in no need of a sacrifice in order to forgive, just as Jesus (pbuh) was in no need of a sacrifice when he forgave using the powers given to him by God.

The Parable of the Vineyard

Jesus (pbuh) told a parable about a man who built a vineyard amongst a certain people. The man left the vineyard, but he sent his servant to the people to receive some of the fruit from the vineyard. However the people of the land rejected the servant's request and they attack him and sent him away. The man who built the vineyard, despite their rejection, sent another of his servants to receive some of the fruit. The town's people attacked him also. Over time, the man sent more and more of his servants. Many were beating and others were killed. So finally that man decided to send his son to do the job, believing that the townspeople might show respect to his son for his father's sake. But they killed his son, as well.

In this story, we understand that the man who built the vineyard was God and the vineyard is his guidance and revelations. Perhaps the fruit that is spoken of is his life or souls on earth (vineyard) and the townspeople are a group of people of the earth. God sends his prophets (servants) to retrieve his souls, but the people reject the prophets. They even kill some of them. So, God sends his son (presumably Jesus) and he falls to the same fate. What should be clear from this story is that mercy and grace are given repeatedly to the SAME PEOPLE. It is obvious that God continuously forgave their transgressions, not because of the prophets' deaths, but in spite of them. Another point to be made is that every prophet, including the son had the same message and agenda. The son was not given a new goal to meet or new methods to follow. It was the same methods, goal and the same results. So the question is what will God do in response to his son's death?

_12:9_ _What shall therefore the lord of the vineyard do? he will come and destroy the husbandmen, and will give the vineyard unto others._

The son's death (Jesus' death) only served as the last straw for God. He does not formulate his son's death into another avenue for forgiveness of their sin. He destroyed them for their sin and he gave their vineyard (guidance) to another people. Through this parable, Jesus' (pbuh) life mission is understood. So too, is the ramifications of his death. It doesn't bring about salvation, but it ends the opportunity for those who rejected him to receive their own prophet and begins an opportunity for another group of people.

It should he emphasized that this story which perpetuates the idea that Jesus (pbuh) had the same message as all other prophets is to be read in conjunction with the story of Jesus (pbuh) and the scribe, to whom Jesus (pbuh) says following the laws is the way to heaven, which occurs in the very same chapter. Also, the prophets of the Old Testament were sent to the Israelites. And according to this parable, so was Jesus (pbuh).

WAS JESUS (pbuh) WORTHY TO BE A SACRIFICE?

Because the qualification of a sacrifice must be sinlessness, Mark disqualifies Jesus (pbuh) when he records that Jesus called the Greek woman, her sick daughter and all non-Jews dogs (7:26-27). Slandering two innocent people, along with racism should suffice, in proving that Jesus (pbuh) was not sinless according to Mark.

CHAPTER V – THE GOSPEL OF LUKE

TO WHOM WAS JESUS' (pbuh) MESSAGE INTENDED?

_24:47_ *And that repentance and remission of sins should be preached in his name among all nations, beginning at Jerusalem.*

It seems that Jesus' (pbuh) message is to all nations according to Luke. We shall see.

JESUS' (pbuh) MESSAGE IN THE GOSPEL OF LUKE?

Faith

There was a sinful woman who came to Jesus (pbuh) and fell before his feet and wept. Perhaps she had heard that he forgave people's sins. The woman was ridiculed for her sins, but Jesus (pbuh) said her sins are forgiven and her faith SAVED her (7:37-50). This very sentiment is echoed in the story of a blind man, who sought Jesus' (pbuh) miraculous healing ability, in spite of those who rebuked him. Jesus (pbuh) said that the man's faith had SAVED him (18:35-43). The faith in which Jesus (pbuh) spoke was faith that Jesus (pbuh) was a man of God. Their faith had absolutely no basis in his death or even his resurrection for that matter. You see, the faith was demonstrated by their actions. By our faith and actions we are judged.

There was another man, by the name of Zaccheus, who clamored to see Jesus (pbuh). Zaccheus was a short man, so he stood in a tree so as to get a glimpse of Jesus (pbuh) when he walked by. Jesus (pbuh) took notice of Zaccheus and told Zaccheus that he must stay in Zaccheus' house. Of course, Zacchues was elated to have Jesus (pbuh) at his home, but others spoke against Jesus (pbuh) staying with a man they deemed a sinner. Upon entering Zaccheus' home, Jesus (pbuh) said "TODAY salvation has entered your home." The salvation that Jesus (pbuh) spoke of was the same salvation he spoke of to the sinful woman and the blind man. Jesus (pbuh) recognized Zaccheus' faith through his actions. It was not a salvation to be administered at a later date, but that very day.

_6:46_ _And why call ye me, Lord, Lord, and do not the things which I say?_

Your faith is demonstrated through your actions. It's quite easy to determine if you have faith in Jesus (pbuh). Just do what he tells you to do. This is the same message every prophet of God has conveyed. And none of them, including Jesus (pbuh), said believe in my death and you will be saved. Jesus (pbuh) never added this to his followers' curriculum.

Follow the Law

11:28 *...blessed are they that hear the word of God, and keep it.*

In chapter 6 of Luke, Jesus (pbuh) gave a list of things you must do in order to reach heaven. It can be summed up with these simple words, "do good deeds and your reward shall be great." The reward he spoke of is forgiveness and Heaven, but what are the good deeds that we must do? Luke records two occasions when someone comes to Jesus (pbuh) in hopes of finding the path to heaven and on both occasions the same answer is given, Follow the laws and commandments of God (10:25-28, 18:18-23).

One question we must ask ourselves is why did these men ask Jesus (pbuh) how to get to heaven, considering that they already knew and followed the laws? I believe that they asked him this question because Jesus' (pbuh) instructing them to love their enemies and turn the other cheek. Jesus (pbuh) was added and extracting from the laws, so they asked him this in order to find out whether they were on the right path or not. And Jesus (pbuh) confirmed that they were on the right path, but that they must go the extra step to become even more righteous. And Jesus (pbuh) told them how to be more righteous. He said follow my words and actions and you will be saved (9:23, 14:27).

Lazarus and the Rich Man

Jesus (pbuh) told a story about a beggar named Lazarus who slept at the gate of a certain rich man's home hoping to get some straps of food or first aid for his wounds. However, Lazarus died and went to heaven, which is called Abraham's (pbuh) bosom in the story. The rich man died as well, but he went to hell. Lazarus could see and speak with the rich man from heaven and vice versa. The rich man felt tormented from the flames of hell, perhaps in the same manner as Lazarus felt in his state of poverty. So he asked Abraham (pbuh) to send Lazarus to get him some water to cool his tongue. Abraham (pbuh) told the rich man that there is a barrier between the two places which cannot be breached. So the rich man began to think about his 5 brothers on earth and their imminent fate in this same place of torment. He asked Abraham (pbuh) to send Lazarus to warn his brothers.

16:29 *Abraham saith unto him, They have Moses and the prophets; let them hear them.*

16:30 *And he said, Nay, father Abraham: but if one went unto them from the dead, they will repent.*

16:31 *And he said unto him, If they hear not Moses and the prophets, neither will they be persuaded, though one rose from the dead.*

There are a number of things that one can take from this parable, but salvation through human sacrifice is not one of them. One thing is that rich people are to share their wealth with the poor. Another is that Jesus (pbuh) seems to be saying that people are destined for hell and heaven because on faith and works and that these works are derived from the teachings of "Moses (pbuh) and the prophets."

This parable suggests that obeying these teachings is sufficient for one to avoid hellfire and to enter heaven. But strangely enough, Jesus (pbuh) did not believe that (Lazarus') resurrection from the dead would convince people to follow the laws of the prophets. And he was correct because the story of his resurrection has only convinced people to not follow the laws of Moses (pbuh), and to only believe in his death and resurrection.

The person perhaps most qualified to tell others what man must do to steer clear of hell is someone who is already in hell. And what does the rich man hope that his brothers do? REPENT!!!!!!!

Repentance and Forgiveness

Jesus (pbuh) wanted his followers to always pray (18:1) and stay steadfast on God's path. Their prayers included a request for forgiveness from God. Those who violate the laws are to repent and be kind to others in order to have their sins forgiven (11:1-4). The gospel according to Luke reinforces the idea of repentance to a much greater degree than Matthew and Mark's gospels.

5:32 *I came not to call the righteous, but sinners to repentance.*

Jesus (pbuh) twice says without repentance, the sinner will perish (13:3, 13:5). He speaks of heaven being more joyful over the repentance of one sinner, than they are over 99 righteous people without need for repentance (15:7,10), which begs another question, are their people without need of repentance? If they are in no need of repentance, they are also in no need of a savior. Of course, the Bible says that all have sinned and fallen short of the grace of God (Romans 3:23). But Luke contradicts this claim.

_1:6_ *And they (Zachariah and Elizabeth) were both righteous before God, walking in all the commandments and ordinances of the Lord blameless.*

This verse nullifies the idea of the Original Sin and the claim that Jesus' (pbuh) death is the only way to salvation, unless we are to believe that you can be righteous, blameless, and adhere to every law of God and God will still punish you. On the contrary, the fact that Zachariah (pbuh) and Elizabeth are called righteous before God helps to solidify Jesus' (pbuh) message that obeying the laws is the path to heaven. Jesus' (pbuh) last recorded words in Luke were not about his death, but about repentance for forgiveness of sins (24:47).

Forgiven and Punished

Throughout my research for this book, I never realized that the Christian doctrine holds that if you sin, God punishes for the sin AND he forgives the sin, until I heard this from Islamic propagator and former Christian, Gary Miller. In the "Lord's prayer" Jesus (pbuh) says:

_11:4_ *And forgive us our sins; for we also forgive every one that is indebted to us.*

Miller asks, "How do you forgive a debt?" If someone owes you $10.00 and you forgive his debt, then he doesn't have to pay you, EVER. But if he pays the debt, then you did not forgive it. Even if someone else pays his debt for him, you did not forgive it. In the words of Miller, "you don't say to the man in debt, 'You know that money you owe me, forget it. Now, give me my money!!!'" In the same vein, God either forgives your sin or you pay for your sin. If he forgives your sin, then no one has to die. If you or someone else (Jesus) pays for your sin, then the sin is not forgiven. However Christians believe that Jesus (pbuh) paid for your sins AND that you are forgiven.

The Prodigal Son

Jesus (pbuh) was great at giving a decree and giving a parable to illustrate his point. Probably Jesus' (pbuh) best known parable is the Prodigal Son. There was a man who had two sons. The older son lived with the father and was very obedient to him. The younger son was more rebellious. He asked that his inheritance be given to him now. He took it and went off into the land. He lived a sinful life and dwelled amongst the lowest of the low. But one day he decided to return to his father. He knows that he is helpless without his father. But he thinks that he is no longer worthy to be his father's son but his father's servant. So he gathers himself and heads back to ask for his father's forgiveness for his departure and his behavior. The father, seeing his son from afar, runs to his son to meet him and he hugs and kisses his son. He gives his son the finest clothing, jewelry and the best food. His elder son feels slated because of the big fuss made over his younger brother. But the father told the elder son, that all he had is his, but it was fitting that they rejoice over his son who "was dead, and is alive again; and was lost, and is found."(15:11-32)

This parable in every way denounces the Christian's understanding of atonement and totally reiterates the teachings of Jesus (pbuh). The father in this story is God, the elder son is the righteous person and the younger son is the sinner. God gives each of them free will to choice to be righteous or to sin. The elder son follows the laws of God and he is on the path to heaven. His younger brother breaks the laws and he is on the path to hell. But as Ezekiel 18:21 says, the sinner turned from his sinful ways and makes his way back to God. And God sees his gesture of repentance and God accepts it joyfully and without haste. And interestingly, the cattle that the father killed for the food is a celebration for the return of the sinner.

It is not a sacrifice in order for him to return. For the Christian doctrine to be correct, the elder son would have had to be sacrificed by the father in order for his younger brother's safe return. And the younger brother must accept his brother's death as the entry fee into the father's household.

WAS JESUS (pbuh) WORTHY TO BE A SACRIFICE?

It is noteworthy that the gospels, which are often times biased biographies of Jesus (pbuh), do not maintain that he was sinless. It is maintained by the other New Testament writers that he was sinless. The writers of the gospels perhaps had a difficult time establishing his sinlessness when some of his recorded actions are to the contrary. For example, Jesus (pbuh) makes it obligatory for his follows to not only forsake everything but him (14:33) but to hate everyone, including themselves.

_14:26_ _If any man come to me, and hate not his father, and mother, and wife, and children, and brethren, and sisters, yea, and his own life also, he cannot be my disciple._

Though one sin is sufficient to prove my point, is it clear that Jesus (pbuh) is guilty of more than one sin in the book of Luke. Though John the Baptist (pbuh) abhors alcohol, it seems Jesus (pbuh) succumbs to its temptation (7:33-34). Perhaps Jesus (pbuh) was not a drunkard, but I would qualify any indulgence in wine to be a sin. And the Bible forbids it for a person of Jesus' (pbuh) stature, at any rate. Jesus (pbuh) himself forbade the use of insults, yet he is himself guilty of calling the Pharisee (11:40) and his very own disciples, fools (24:25) in the book of Luke.

CHAPTER VI – THE GOSPEL OF JOHN

The gospel of John demands an explanation before delving into its text. It is a radically different biography of Jesus (pbuh) compared to its counterparts. The other gospels make it a point to portray Jesus (pbuh) as the Messiah of the Jews, while John is infatuated with Jesus (pbuh) being a deity. If you believe that Jesus (pbuh) is the Messiah, or anointed by God, you are more inclined to evaluate his teachings. If you believe him to be God, then you will begin to focus on his person. In order to correlate these two depictions by the gospels, many Christians deemed it necessary to equate the Messiah with God, which was never understood to be the case by the Jews, nor do they at the present moment await a God/Messiah.

John's gospel was written after the other three gospels and it was addressed to gentile Christians. That's right! The people John was attempting to engage were already followers of the teachings of Jesus (pbuh). Perhaps they used the other gospels as inspiration. John's goal to establish the divinity of Jesus (pbuh) means that before his gospel, there was a lack of support for Jesus' (pbuh) divinity and he chose to fill that void. And he did. If ever you met a Christian and you ask him about Jesus (pbuh), he with almost always skip the first three gospels and go to John to describe Jesus (pbuh) as God and God's son.

John's very first objective is to equate Jesus (pbuh) with God and attribute the creation of everything to him (John 1:3) and he does so immediately in this book. John frequently uses the words "the Jews" to describe the people in opposition to Jesus (pbuh), whereas the other gospels describe these people as the hierarchy of their faith, the scribes and Pharisees. John's gospel is set in Galilee, whereas the other gospels are in Judea. John has very important details of Jesus' (pbuh) life which are exclusive to his gospel, like Jesus' (pbuh) first miracle (2:1-11), the woman at the well (4:6-30) and the raising of Lazarus (11:1-44). The other gospels say Jesus (pbuh) used parables to give his messages, John has Jesus (pbuh) using regular conversation to deliver his message. The gospel of John has fewer miracles, fewer Old Testament prophecies, and fewer parables than all the other gospels. And he has fewer sermons than all but Mark, yet John's gospel is the most dogmatic. Only John has the seven famous "I am" saying of Jesus (pbuh). He gives seven miracles of Jesus as well, but the sole purpose of his miracles is to signify Jesus' (pbuh) divinity. And last but not least, John separates Moses' (pbuh) law from Jesus (pbuh), giving the impression that the laws of Moses (pbuh) are obsolete.

__1:17__ For the law was given by Moses, but grace and truth came by Jesus Christ.

The truth of the matter is that grace and truth came by Jesus Christ (pbuh), who taught that grace and truth came by the laws of Moses (pbuh). So the laws were not obsolete as John insinuates, but they were in cohesion with the teachings of Jesus (pbuh) and they were to be adhered to in conjunction with those teachings.

FOR WHOM WAS JESUS' (pbuh) MESSAGE INTENDED?

_10:16_ _I have other sheep which are not of this fold; I must bring them also._

John, unlike the other gospels, leaves little to the imagination in the case of Jesus (pbuh) intended audience when his gospel says the world is to hear the message of Jesus (pbuh) (3:16-17). But he also said that salvation is for the Jews (4:22). What is more confusing is that in this very same chapter, Jesus (pbuh) is called the savior of the world (4:42). It seems contradictory to say whomever believes in him will have everlasting life and for Jesus (pbuh) to say that salvation is for a particular group. Jesus (pbuh) preached to Jews and all his disciples were Jews. Perhaps the truth is that Jesus' (pbuh) message will be heard throughout the world and whoever believes him amongst the Jews will be saved. We will soon get to the bottom of this matter.

JESUS' (pbuh) MESSAGE IN THE GOSPEL OF JOHN?

_1:29_ _The next day John seeth Jesus coming unto him, and saith, Behold the Lamb of God, which taketh away the sin of the world._

John's gospel is the only gospel which records these words of John the

Baptist (pbuh). Why is that? Did all the other gospel writers forget this quote from John the Baptist? Or is the writer of John embellishing his story about John the Baptist and Jesus (pbut)? John's gospel also says that Jesus (pbuh) baptized John the Baptist (pbuh) (3:22-24). It is unfathomable that the other gospel writers forgot such an important event. All the gospels tell that Jesus (pbuh) was to succeed John the Baptist (pbuh) and that Jesus' (pbuh) baptism would be on a higher scale than John the Baptist's (pbuh). But Matthew and Mark's gospel have Jesus (pbuh) being baptized by John (pbuh). Jesus (pbuh) actually baptizing the Baptist would be a dramatic scene. This passing of the torch would be a great symbolic gesture of his succession to John the Baptist (pbuh), which is too significant to omit. But the reason the other gospels do not have this event is because John the Baptist (pbuh) was in prison when both his and Jesus' (pbuh) alleged baptism was to take place (Luke 3:16-22). This is according to Luke who testifies that he is giving an orderly account of the life of Jesus (pbuh) (Luke 1:3). So, it appears that the writer of John's gospel was a bit overzealous when discussing John the Baptist (pbuh). And Mark and Matthew have mistakenly stated that John (pbuh) baptized Jesus (pbuh), when it was physically impossible for him to do so.

To further accentuate the point that this declaration by John is probably embellished is that it specifically states that John the Baptist (pbuh) recognized Jesus (pbuh) as the lamb taking away sin and the son of God (John 1:34), yet Matthew and Luke say that John the Baptist (pbuh) had only heard of Jesus (pbuh) while John (pbuh) was in prison (Matt 11:2-3, Luke 7:18-20). These gospels record John the Baptist (pbuh) asking his disciples to find out if Jesus (pbuh) is "the one that they have been waiting for." So how could either of them have baptized the other when they had never met? Because of the conflicting reports on John the Baptist (pbuh) and his interactions with Jesus (pbuh), it cannot be conclusively stated that John the Baptist (pbuh) actually said that Jesus (pbuh) would "take away the sin of the world."

John is the only gospel to maintain that Jesus (pbuh) is the Lamb of God.

And John changes the time of the crucifixion. Mark says that the Last Supper was the day of the Passover Meal and Jesus (pbuh) was tried and crucified the next morning at 9 o'clock (Mark 15:25). John says Jesus (pbuh) was sentenced to death on the Day of Preparation for the Passover at noon (John 19:14). "Why, then, did John-our latest Gospel-change the day and time when Jesus died? It may be because in John's gospel, Jesus is the Passover lamb, whose sacrifice brings salvation from sins. Exactly like the Passover Lamb, Jesus has to die on the day (the Day of Preparation) and the time (sometime after noon) when the Passover lambs were being slaughtered in the Temple. In other words, John changed the historical datum in order to make a theological point: Jesus is the sacrificial lamb." (Bart Ehrman, "Jesus, Interrupted") It is abundantly clear that John has altered events in order to satisfy his own agenda and not simply present the evidence as he knew it.

Follow Me

20:30 *And many other signs truly did Jesus in the presence of his disciples, which are not written in this book:*

20:31 *But these are written, that ye might believe that Jesus is the Christ, the Son of God; and that believing ye might have life through his name.*

John unapologetically admits to his motives. He purposely omitted events of Jesus' (pbuh) life in order to focus on the identity of Jesus (pbuh). Despite John's callous approach to a biography of Jesus (pbuh), it is still possible to derive Jesus' (pbuh) message to his followers. In the other gospels, Jesus (pbuh) asks his followers to be like children. John says his followers are to be "born again" or "generated from above" meaning that they are to start anew, start from the beginning and begin living their life as he instructs them to (3:3). The fact that Jesus (pbuh) believed the ideal person to emulate for salvation is a child or baby, debunks the Original Sin concept, which states you are helplessly cursed from Adam's (pbuh) sin and in need of redemption by Jesus' (pbuh) blood. In fact, Jesus (pbuh) plainly said that his WORDS actually saved his followers (5:34). The famous John 3:16 says whoever believes in Jesus (pbuh) is saved, not whoever believes in his death is saved.

And Jesus (pbuh) is presented with an opportunity in John to tell his followers that it is incumbent upon them to believe in his death and resurrection in order to be saved, but what does he say?

6:40 *And this is the will of him that sent me, that every one which seeth the Son, and believeth on him, may have everlasting life: and I will raise him up at the last day...*

6:47 *Verily, verily, I say unto you, He that believeth on me hath everlasting life.*

If you were amongst the people who surrounded Jesus (pbuh), how could you have deduced that he meant believe in his death and resurrection to be granted heaven? You couldn't. Some may say that Jesus (pbuh) in this instance meant that his followers are to believe in every aspect of Jesus' (pbuh) life in order to be saved and I totally agree with this premise, because if you believe in every aspect of Jesus' (pbuh) life, you will undoubtedly find that his death was of little importance to his mission. It is Paul who said his death and resurrection is the cornerstone of Christianity, and without them Jesus' (pbuh) entire teachings are of no effect (1Cor. 15:17). Even after Jesus (pbuh) was supposed to be resurrected, he never ever said believe in my death and resurrection to be saved or anything of that nature. Jesus (pbuh) wants his followers to believe in his words.

8:51 *Verily, verily, I say unto you, If a man keep my saying, he shall never see death.*

14:15 *If ye love me, keep my commandments.*

Jesus' (pbuh) final message to his disciples was "FOLLOW ME, FOLLOW ME" (21:19, 22). How do you follow him by following a religion ABOUT him, and not his way of life and mission? In a nutshell, I would say Jesus' (pbuh) message in the gospel of John is "I am the way, pick up your cross and follow me." But was Jesus (pbuh) successful in conveying that message? Probably the most damaging words to the idea of salvation by Jesus' (pbuh) blood are found in John.

17:3 *And this is life eternal, that they might know thee the only true God, and Jesus Christ, whom thou hast sent.*

17:4 *I have glorified thee on the earth: I have finished the work which thou gavest me to do.*

17:5 *And now, O Father, glorify thou me with thine own self with the glory which I had with thee before the world was.*

Jesus (pbuh) plainly says that the way to God is by knowing him and knowing God. His job was to glorify God and he has FINISHED the work that he was given to do, and now he asks for his reward. This is well before the supposed crucifixion. He did not say that he has completed the first portion of his work. He said that he finished "the" work which he was given. Therefore crucifixion was not in his job description and it is not a requirement for him to complete or for his followers to believe.

What is interesting is that John records Jesus' (pbuh) last words on the cross as "It is finished." Some Christians take this to mean that he has finished that job that he was sent to do. If they take this view, then they are saying that his resurrection was not a part of his job. Also, due to the apparent discrepancy in Jesus (pbuh) finishing his job twice, many Bibles use the word "completed" for one verse of John and "finished" for the other verse, so the reader will not correlate the two verses. Unfortunately, the words have the very same meaning, so we are forced to conclude that Jesus (pbuh) finished his job twice or one of these stories is not accurate. This leaves the reader the option to decide which statement he believes to be the correct one.

WAS JESUS (pbuh) WORTHY TO BE A SACRIFICE?

Despite the laws' strict punishment towards those who mistreat their parents, Jesus' (pbuh) contempt for his parents is documented as being present from childhood. In the gospel of Luke, Jesus' (pbuh) mother and father were frantically searching for him, when he wandered off as a 12 year old boy. Coldly, Jesus (pbuh) shrugs their sorrows off.

Luke 2:49 *And he said unto them, How is it that ye sought me? Wist ye not that I must be about my Father's business?*

Luke 2:50 *And they understood not the saying which he spake unto them.*

Is it ever appropriate to ask your parents, "Why are you looking for me?" especially after you have wandered off? Jesus (pbuh) seems to be saying that his parents knew about his mission from God, but Luke says that they did not understand him, so his hostility towards them is unjustified. Because he was only 12 years old, this may not be construed as a sin, but it apparently led to another episode, where Jesus (pbuh) insulted his mother in John's gospel.

Jesus (pbuh) and his mother were at a wedding in Cana in Galilee and the people there ran short of wine. Jesus' (pbuh) mother now grasped the understanding that Jesus (pbuh) had miraculous powers, so she asked Jesus (pbuh) to give them more wine.

2:4 *Jesus saith unto her, Woman, what have I to do with thee? Mine hour is not yet come.*

Jesus (pbuh) eventually replenishes their wine and it is described by John to be the very first miracle of Jesus (pbuh) (2:11). So Jesus (pbuh) aids and abets the sin of alcohol consumption.

Habakkuk 2:15 *Woe unto him that giveth his neighbour drink, that puttest thy venom thereto, and makest him drunken...*

And is it not disrespectful to say to your mother, "WOMAN, what do you want?" The answer is obviously yes. But what is strange is now he says that his time is not yet, when Luke says that at the age of 12 he was delivering his message. And did Jesus (pbuh) not know the word for "mother" in Aramaic? Of course, he did. He used the word on numerous occasions. One time in particular was when Jesus (pbuh) was on the cross speaking to his mother Mary.

_19:26-27_ _Jesus saw his own mother, and the disciple standing near whom he loved, he said to his mother, "Woman, behold your son." Then he said to the disciple, "Behold your mother." And from that hour, he took his mother into his family._

Jesus (pbuh) calls his mother "woman" again on the cross, but he says she is the "mother" of his disciple. Jesus (pbuh) called God his father, but his mother he calls "woman," insinuating that she is beneath him. This is the same way that the gospel of John says that Jesus (pbuh) addressed the woman caught in adultery.

_8:10_ _When Jesus had lifted up himself, and saw none but the woman, he said unto her, Woman, where are those thine accusers? hath no man condemned thee?_

Jesus' (pbuh) Mistakes?

John records Jesus (pbuh) making many contradictory remarks. These remarks may be used to counter the argument that Jesus (pbuh) is God, because that would mean that one of the statements contrary to another must be a lie or an untruth. If we conclude that Jesus (pbuh) was a man, the discrepancies may be seen as an intentional deceit or simply a mistake. Or we can conclude that John is the person in error, giving room to doubt the entire gospel account. Here is an example of Jesus' (pbuh) errors.

_3:13_ _And no man hath ascended up to heaven, but he that came down from heaven, even the Son of man which is in heaven._

Jesus (pbuh) says no man has been to heaven but him, yet the Bible tells of Enoch (Gen. 5:24), Elijah (pbuh) (2Kings 2:11) and someone acquainted with Paul (2Cor. 12:2-4) going up to heaven. That means that people went to heaven before and after Jesus (pbuh). Another problem is that Jesus (pbuh) is the "son of man," yet he says that the son of man is in heaven as he was on earth speaking to Nicodemus.

Also the "son of man" denotes his humanity and not his supposed godly nature. Therefore this statement is contradictory because if this were at all true, the son of man Jesus (pbuh) would be on earth and the son of God Jesus (pbuh) was in heaven. Is Jesus (pbuh) or John confused?

Within two chapters, Jesus (pbuh) says he has lost none of his disciples other than the son of perdition, Judas (17:12) and then Jesus (pbuh) says he has lost none, period (18:9). Both of these statements cannot be true. Also in John 16:5, Jesus (pbuh) says that none of his disciples have asked him where he is going. Yet, Peter (13:36) and Thomas (14:5) both asked Jesus (pbuh) where he is going and he responded to them.

Jesus (pbuh) the Dishonest?

In light of the ridicule Jesus (pbuh) had for the Pharisees, it is noteworthy that John records a Pharisee catching Jesus (pbuh) in a lie. Jesus (pbuh) said "If I bear witness of myself, my witness is not true" in 5:31. However, Jesus (pbuh) changes his tone a little later.

_8:12_ *Then spake Jesus again unto them, saying, I am the light of the world: he that followeth me shall not walk in darkness, but shall have the light of life.*

_8:13_ *The Pharisees therefore said unto him, Thou bearest record of thyself; thy record is not true.*

_8:14_ *Jesus answered and said unto them, Though I bear record of myself, yet my record is true: for I know whence I came, and whither I go; but ye cannot tell whence I come, and whither I go.*

The translators of John, as they did with "finished" and "completed", change the words from "witness" to "record," in order to cover this discrepancy, but again the words have the same meaning in this context. And any Bible, which provides reference verses, gives 8:14 as a reference to 5:31. What is peculiar is that Jesus (pbuh) does not deny, but confirm the claim of the Pharisee, giving the indication that he is intentional contradicting his previous statement. Because two exact opposite things cannot be true, we must ask which statement was the truth? The answer is insignificant with respect to this book. I must only prove that one of them is false.

CHAPTER VII – MY CONCLUSION OF JESUS' AUDIENCE, MESSAGE AND WORTHINESS

It is extremely important for me to point out that I do not believe Jesus (pbuh) was guilty of the sins attributed to him. I find it hard to believe that a man appointed by God would call people dogs and pigs or be disrespectful to innocent people. I do not believe he drank wine or that he contributed to the drinking of wine by anyone else. The reason that I listed the gospels' account of the sins of Jesus (pbuh) was only to demonstrate that according to the Biblical description of Jesus (pbuh), he is unqualified as a sinless sacrifice.

He is even in need of anger management. He declares that anger for no good reason is a sin (Matt 5:22), yet he shows anger when he was questioned about healing on the Sabbath (Mark 3:5). He uses a whip to clear the temple (John 2:14-16). He gives a parable of a king having his enemies killed before him (Luke 19:12-27), which infers his use of vengeance in this world or the next world. And he curses a tree to wither and die because he was HUNGRY and it did not produce fruit, OUT OF SEASON (Mark 11:12-14). Apologists attempt to justify this act by saying that Jesus (pbuh) was using the tree as a symbol for the Jewish people who did not bear fruit or show righteousness. The problem is that Jesus (pbuh) did not symbolically kill the tree. He literally killed it and the reason given had nothing to do with the people of Israel and their actions, and everything to do with his hunger.

According to Christianity and in light of all the sins recorded in the gospels, Jesus (pbuh) is himself in need of a savior. This may explain why the Gospels say that he was baptized, as the sinners were, cleansing himself of his own sin by John the Baptist (pbuh) in the first place. The writer of John's gospel perhaps sensing the dilemma of a baptized Jesus (pbuh), by a man who seems to be a bit more righteous than Jesus (pbuh), inserts the story of the baptism of John the Baptist (pbuh) (a non-gluttonous and non-wine drinking man). Nonetheless, Jesus (pbuh) is not a sinless man in the Bible and therefore his death would not be sufficient for the salvation of mankind as understood by Christian doctrine.

The most difficult answer to be found is to whom was Jesus' (pbuh) message intended? The gospels in most instances seem to suggest that it was for the entire world to hear. However, on a few occasions, Jesus (pbuh) explicitly stated that he was only sent to the lost sheep of the house of Israel. It is maintained by Christians that he was sent to them first, then to the rest of the world. Matthew, like a thorn in their side, continues to betray the Christian belief that Jesus' (pbuh) message was universal.

Matthew 25:32-33 *All the nations will be gathered before him, and he will separate the people one from another as a shepherd separates the sheep from the goats. He will put the sheep on his right and the goats on his left.*

This verse presents a problem, because the sheep are the Jews (Micah 2:12, Matt. 10:6-7, Matt. 15:24), and those of them who reject Jesus (pbuh) are the goats. But if Jesus (pbuh) is judging "all the nations," he must be judging gentiles, as well. So where do they fit in? Gentiles are not the sheep, because even believing gentiles are dogs (Matt. 15:25-26, Mark 7:27). But Jesus (pbuh) says "I lay down My life for the sheep." (John 10:11, 15), so this forces Christians to maintain that the believing gentiles are sheep, as well, despite a lack of evidence in support of this claim. But what does Jesus (pbuh) mean when he says "all nations?" The gospel which seems to say the least about Jesus' (pbuh) intended audience gives us a little more insight into this question.

Luke 24:47 *And that repentance and remission of sins should be preached in his name among all nations, beginning at Jerusalem.*

If we read this verse carefully, it appears that Jesus (pbuh) is describing the land of the Palestine as "all nations." When he says start in Jerusalem, this indicates that he is considering Jerusalem as a nation, when it is actually a city. When Jesus (pbuh) speaks of sheep from another fold in John 10:16, he is still talking about Jews. But it is the Jews of another city. In Acts 1:8, Jesus (pbuh) is said to have added two other names to the list. Jesus (pbuh) tells his disciples to be his witnesses in Jerusalem, Judea and Samaria and all over the world. Again, Jesus (pbuh) is telling his disciples to witness throughout Palestine, as Judea and Samaria are what is now known as the West Bank. This idea that the land of Palestine is the whole world has long been implicated by Biblical authors. The story of Noah's (pbuh) ark speaks of a flood which covered the "face of the earth," but this is understood by some scholars to mean only the land of Noah (pbuh). This suggests that the writer/s of the Pentateuch considered the land inhabited by Jews to be the only place worthy of recognition. Upon reading the Jewish Torah, you will find that this understanding doesn't warrant any stretch of the imagination, due to the almost total disregard of any beings on earth besides the ancestors of the Israelites. Add to this the fact that Jesus (pbuh) is recorded as calling the Israelites children and regarding the non-Jews as dogs and pigs. The other two synoptic gospels seem to agree that Jesus (pbuh) sent his disciples to all nations.

Matthew 28:19 *Go ye therefore, and teach all nations,*

Mark 16:15 *And he said unto them, Go ye into all the world, and preach the gospel to every creature…*

Mark 16:20 *And they went forth, and preached every where, the Lord working with them, and confirming the word with signs following. Amen.*

Mark's gospel says that they PREACHED EVERYWHERE. But were these nations of Palestine or nations of the world, which would include gentiles? The book of Acts was written by the same author of the gospel of Luke. Luke says that Jesus' (pbuh) parting words to his disciples were to "preach to all nations," but Luke says that Peter later saw a vision which instructed him to preach to GENTILES (Acts 10:11-11:1). In fact, Peter says that it was UNLAWFUL for Jews to even keep company with gentiles (Acts 10:28) before he saw this vision. But if Jesus (pbuh) had instructed them to teach gentiles after he was raised from the dead and "they went forth preaching everywhere" and "to every creature," this epiphany of Peter and the other disciples would have been unnecessary. Did they simply forget that Jesus (pbuh) had already told them to go to the whole world? Did they also forget that they HAD ALREADY begun preaching to the whole world? Of course not. If your adored teacher comes back from the dead and tells you to do something and you do it, it's pretty safe to say, you did not forget what he said and what you did. Therefore it can be deduced that Jesus (pbuh) meant by all nations, all Jewish cities or that he did not say these words attributed to him, at all. In either case, it is apparent that Jesus' (pbuh) message as he unambiguously stated was only for Jews (Matt. 15:24) and his mission was altered after his life on earth.

Along with Zachariah's (pbuh) claim that John the Baptist (pbuh) and Jesus were to help Israel fulfill the covenant between Abraham (pbuh) and God (Luke 1:68-80), here are other quotations from the gospel writers which give more insight into Jesus' (pbuh) intended audience.

Matthew 1:21 And she shall bring forth a son, and thou shalt call his name JESUS: for he shall save his people from their sins.

John 11:51 And this spake he not of himself: but being high priest that year, he prophesied that Jesus should die for that nation;

John 11:52 And not for that nation only, but that also he should gather together in one the children of God that were scattered abroad.

John 17:9 I pray for them: I pray not for the world, but for them which thou hast given me; for they are thine.

Acts 13:23 Of this man's seed hath God according to his promise raised unto Israel a Saviour, Jesus

I must mention that Peter's vision, not only made it permissible to teach to gentiles, but the vision made it permissible to eat foods deemed by the Torah to be unclean, such as swine. Of course, this is an example of those who teach men to disobey the laws of Moses (pbuh). And by doing so, they are disobeying the words of Jesus (pbuh), no matter what their vision was. Oddly enough, the book of Isaiah is often cited as a book of prophecies and its final chapter makes a prophecy about God catching people committing sins at the end of times. One of those sins will be eating swine (Isa. 66:17-18). Therefore Peter's vision misguided him, as any vision would if it is in direct conflict with the words of a prophet of God. Yet Peter is not alone in misguidance.

AFTER Peter is said to have received his vision to preach to gentiles, Paul is FORBIDDEN from preaching in the land of Asia by the Holy Spirit (Acts 16:6). There is no mention of why the Holy Spirit would contradict Jesus' (pbuh) command to preach to every nation. The only logical explanation would be that the Holy Spirit and Jesus (pbuh) wanted the message to only reach the nations of Palestine. Nevertheless, Paul, without hint of a retraction from the Holy Spirit, took the liberty to preach to the lands of Asia anyway (Acts 19:10, Gal 1:19). The passage in Acts 16:6 does not say that the Holy Spirit told Paul to wait until later to preach to the land of Asia, it says that the Holy Spirit FORBAD it. This is similar to the situation Christian face when Jesus (pbuh) said he is ONLY SENT to the lost sheep. A choice must be made. Do we accept the words of Paul or the words of Jesus (pbuh) and the Holy Spirit?

It should also raise some concerns that Jesus (pbuh) spent over 3 years with his disciples, yet he waits until after his death to tell his disciples to teach the world. The same disciples who could not understand a word he said, the same disciples that lacked faith (Matt. 16:8), that continuously fell asleep as he prayed for his life to be saved (Mark 14:41), that deserted him in his time of need (Mark 14:50), that denied even knowing him (Mark 14:71), that he described as fools even up to his ascension into heaven (Luke 24:25). Jesus' (pbuh) entire life mission was replaced by the words of the resurrected Jesus (pbuh), the message Peter received from a vision from heaven (Acts 10:11-11:9), the vision of Paul and the dreams of John in the book of Revelations.

It is obvious that Jesus' (pbuh) message and the religion of Christianity are not cohesive. Christianity's foundation of Original sin, Jesus' (pbuh) blood for atonement, renouncing of the laws of Moses (pbuh) and belief in Jesus' (pbuh) death and resurrection for salvation are found in the minds of those who claim to have been supernaturally instructed by

Jesus (pbuh) or by God. Why must he instruct you supernaturally, when he was here in the physically form to instruct? And if God or Jesus (pbuh) were to speak to man supernaturally, wouldn't it make sense to reinforce his message, instead of giving an entirely different message. Jesus (pbuh) spoke of those who will hold him in high reverence, but they are not his true followers.

Matthew 7:21 *Not every one that saith unto me, Lord, Lord, shall enter into the kingdom of heaven; but he that doeth the will of my Father which is in heaven.*

Matthew 7:22 *Many will say to me in that day, Lord, Lord, have we not prophesied in thy name? and in thy name have cast out devils? and in thy name done many wonderful works?*

Matthew 7:23 *And then will I profess unto them, I never knew you: depart from me, ye that work iniquity.*

These people are rebuked by Jesus (pbuh) because they do not follow "the will of (the) Father." Adhering to other doctrines contrary to the doctrine taught in the gospel of Jesus (pbuh), though you believe in Jesus (pbuh) sincerely, qualifies you as one shunned by your Lord.

There are numerous occasions in which Jesus (pbuh) speaks of the gospel he taught (Matt. 4:23, 24:14, 26:13, Mark 13:10, 14:9, 16:15, Luke 7:22, 9:6, 20:1). It must be noted that the gospel in which Jesus (pbuh) speaks is not the gospels in the Bible, because they were not written until many years after his death. The gospel or good news is not his death and supposed resurrection, but his teachings. Though we do not have the gospel of Jesus (pbuh), we can use the gospels we have to come to some understanding of his gospel. There are some clear cut says of Jesus (pbuh) on why he came.

__Mark 1:38__ And he said unto them, Let us go into the next towns, that I may preach there also: for therefore came I forth.

__Luke 4:43__ And he said unto them, I must preach the kingdom of God to other cities also: for therefore am I sent.

__Matthew 5:17__ Think not that I am come to destroy the law, or the prophets: I am not come to destroy, but to fulfil.

__Matthew 9:13__ But go ye and learn what that meaneth, I will have mercy, and not sacrifice: for I am not come to call the righteous, but sinners to repentance.

__Matthew 10:34__ Think not that I am come to send peace on earth: I came not to send peace, but a sword.

__Matthew 18:11__ For the Son of man is come to save that which was lost.

__Luke 12:49__ I am come to send fire on the earth;

__Luke 12:51__ Suppose ye that I am come to give peace on earth? I tell you, Nay; but rather division

These declarations clearly define Jesus' (pbuh) mission, yet none of them speak of his death for the payment of sins. Jesus (pbuh) did constantly speak of his death in the Bible, but it is only emphasized in the gospels as an event which he foretold, not as a necessity for heaven. Malcolm X and Martin Luther King both foresaw their deaths, but belief in their deaths have very little to do with their message to people. Both men died in pursuit of civil and human rights for all people, but especially black people who were denied these rights. Yet it is not incumbent upon anyone to believe in their deaths to achieve this goal. The idea is to use the methods they offered to gain civil and human rights and to understand that these goals are worth fighting for, with your time, wealth, resources and even your life.

Jesus' (pbuh) mission was for the repentance and revitalization of righteousness of Jews, and his death sentence was a result of this mission, not the purpose of it. Reading the biographies of Jesus (pbuh) makes this obvious and any further examination of his actual words and actions will reveal this. So when Jesus (pbuh) says his blood will be shed for people's forgiveness of sin, it's no different than saying a Muslim propagator died for people's submission to God. Belief in the death of either person is not obligatory to have forgiveness of sins or for someone to submit to God. It is merely a proclamation that the person died for the belief of this cause, the cause of truth. Thus we are to believe in the truth, not in the death for truth. The truth gives us salvation. Martyrdom is but a testimony of one's dedication to that truth.

CHAPTER VIII – EVIDENCE AGAINST THE CRUCIFIXION

CONFLICTING DETAILS OF THE EVENT

Up to this point, my purpose was to show that even if Jesus (pbuh) was crucified, that in no way was his death or his resurrection a means for salvation. This has been proven from a purely moral standpoint, from the Hebrew Scriptures and from the actual words of Jesus (pbuh). I will now focus on the events leading to and surrounding the alleged crucifixion of Jesus (pbuh). For those unfamiliar with the death of Jesus (pbuh), I will give a brief overview of this event.

Jesus (pbuh) ate his last supper with the disciples, at which point he said that one of them would betray him. The disciple which betrayed Jesus (pbuh) was Judas Iscariot. For thirty pieces of silver this disciple, who had witnessed numerous miracles of Jesus (pbuh) and had himself performed miracles, promised to give Jesus (pbuh) up to the authorities.

After eating, Jesus (pbuh) went into a garden to pray. As Jesus (pbuh) prayed, Judas brought the authorities to capture Jesus (pbuh). They take Jesus (pbuh) in the middle of the night to Pontius Pilate, the Roman overseer of the Jews, Herod, and to Caiaphas, the high priest. None of them find fault with Jesus (pbuh), but the Jewish hierarchy were persistent in wanting to have Jesus (pbuh) killed, so they convinced Pilate to have Jesus (pbuh) crucified. Jesus (pbuh) was beaten and eventually put on the cross and killed. He was taken off of the cross, put in a sepulcher and three days later he is raised from the dead. At which point he appears to his disciples and then he ascends to heaven.

It must be emphasized that the four gospels' account of Jesus'(pbuh) preparation for death, his apprehension, his trial, his death and his resurrection are IMPOSSIBLE to be completely pieced together to tell a coherent story. In order to tell the story of Jesus' (pbuh) death, it is obligatory to pick and choose pieces from each gospel because there are so many discrepancies between the gospel accounts. To illustrate the problem one would have in telling the story of Jesus (pbuh) lasts days, I will give a list of some discrepancies between the gospel writers' and the apostle's account of the events surrounding the crucifixion.

Luke 22:3-23 Satan entered Judas before the last supper.

John 13:27 Satan entered Judas during the last supper.

Luke 22:3-6 Judas met with the chief priests and captains before the Passover meal to betray Jesus (pbuh).

John 13:27-30 After the meal, Judas conspired to betray Jesus (pbuh).

Matthew 26:39 Jesus (pbuh) prayed to God to save him from the crucifixion.

83

John 12:27 Jesus (pbuh) said that he would not pray to be saved from this death, since he was ordained to be crucified.

Matthew 26:34, Luke 22:34 and **John 13:38** Jesus (pbuh) said that Peter will deny knowing him three times for the cock crows once.

Mark 14:30 Jesus (pbuh) said that Peter will deny knowing him three times before the cock crowed twice.

Matthew 26:69-74 Peter made his denial to a damsel or maid, then "another maid" and then to "they that stood by."

Mark 14:66-68 Peter made his denial to the same maid twice, then to "those that stood by."

Luke 22:56-57 Peter made his denial to a maid, then "another" maid, then to "another" maid.

John 18:17, 25, 26 Peter made his denial of Jesus (pbuh) to a "damsel," "they" and to "one of the servants of the high priest."

Matthew 26:48-50 Judas identified Jesus (pbuh) with a kiss.

John 18:3-8 Judas, the band of men and the officers all fell to the ground as Jesus (pbuh) was identifying himself to them.

Matthew 27:5 Judas threw away his bribe money and hanged himself from the grief of his betrayal.

Acts 1:18 Judas used the money to buy a field, in which he fell headlong and was killed from being disemboweled.

Luke 23:7-11 Jesus (pbuh) had a hearing before Herod (which no other gospel mentions).

John 18:13-24 Jesus (pbuh) had a hearing before Annas (which no other gospel mentions).

Matthew 26:59-66, Mark 14:55-64, and Luke 22:66-71 Jesus (pbuh) went before the Sanhedrin.

John 18:13 Jesus (pbuh) did not go before the Sanhedrin.

Matthew 26:63-64 Jesus (pbuh) was asked by the High priest if he was the son of God and Jesus said "you say that."

Mark 14:61 Jesus (pbuh) was questioned by the High priest was he the son of God and Jesus said "I am."

Luke 22:70 Jesus (pbuh) was questioned by the High priest if he was the son of God and Jesus said "you say that I am."

John 18:13 Jesus (pbuh) was not questioned by the high priest.

Matthew 27:11-12, Mark 15:-5 and Luke 23:3-4 Jesus (pbuh) was questioned by Pontius Pilate if he was the King of the Jews and Jesus (pbuh) said "you have said so." And Jesus (pbuh) did not answer anymore of Pilates questions.

John 18:33-37 Jesus (pbuh) was questioned by Pontius Pilate if he was the King of the Jews and Jesus (pbuh) asked him "Do you say this on your own accord or did you get this allegation from hearsay?" And Jesus (pbuh) went on to answer Pilate's other questions.

Matthew 27:27-28 *Jesus (pbuh) was given a scarlet robe to wear by the Roman soldiers.*

Mark 15:16-17 *and* **John 19:2** *Jesus (pbuh) was given a purple robe to wear by the Roman soldiers.*

Luke 23:11 *Jesus (pbuh) was given a robe (no color is mentioned) to wear by Herod and his soldiers.*

Matthew 27:31-32 *and* **Mark 15:20-21** *Simon carried the cross for Jesus (pbuh).*

Luke 23:26 *Simon carried the cross after Jesus (pbuh) did.*

John 19:17 *Jesus (pbuh) carried his own cross.*

Matthew 27:55, **Mark 15:40** *and* **Luke 23:49** *Many women, including Mary Magdalene and Mary mother of James and Joses saw Jesus (pbuh) from afar.*

John 19:25-27 *The women are so close to Jesus (pbuh) that he can converse with them. And in John's gospel only, we find that Jesus' (pbuh) mother was amongst the women at the cross.*

Matthew 27:45 *and* **Luke 23:44** *The sixth and the ninth hour pass while Jesus (pbuh) was on the cross.*

Mark 15:25 *Jesus (pbuh) was put on the cross on the third hour and the sixth and ninth hour passes while Jesus was on the cross.*

John 19:14-15 *Jesus (pbuh) was put on the cross after the sixth hour.*

Matthew 27:44 and *Mark 15:32* Both of the people crucified with Jesus (pbuh) mocked him.

Luke 23:39-42 One person mocked Jesus (pbuh) and the other person defended him.

Matthew 27:46 Jesus (pbuh) spoke in Hebrew "Eli, Eli lama sabachthani?" on the cross.

Mark 15:34 Jesus (pbuh) spoke Aramaic, "Eloi, Eloi, lama sabachthani?" on the cross.

Matthew 27:50-51 and *Mark 15:37-38* Jesus (pbuh) died before the veil of the temple was torn.

Luke 23:45-46 The veil was torn, then Jesus (pbuh) died.

Matthew 27:51-53 records an earthquake, graves opening and people rising from the dead and roaming the city at the time of Jesus' (pbuh) death.

The other three gospels do not mention this tremendous event.

Matthew 28:1-4 There were guards at Jesus' (pbuh) sepulcher.

No other gospel makes mention of these guards.

Matthew 28:1 Mary Magdalene and "the other Mary" went to Jesus' *(pbuh) sepulcher.*

Mark 16:1 *Mary Magdalene, Mary mother of James and Salome went to Jesus' (pbuh) sepulcher.*

Luke 23:55-24:10 *Mary Magdalene, Joanna, Mary the mother of James, and "other women" went to Jesus' (pbuh) sepulcher.*

John 20:1 *Mary Magdalene alone went to the sepulcher.*

Mark 16:2 *The two women went to the sepulcher after sunrise.*

John 20:1 *Mary Magdalene went alone and it was still dark.*

Matthew 28:1-2 *The stone of the sepulcher was still at the entrance of the sepulcher when the women arrived.*

Mark 16:4 *The stone was already rolled away when the women arrived.*

Matthew 28:2 *There was an earthquake (only in Matthew's account) and an angel came down to earth, rolled the stone away from the entrance and sat on the stone*

Mark 16:5 *There was a young man sitting inside of the sepulcher*

Luke 24:3-4 *There were two men standing inside of the sepulcher.*

John 20:12 *There were two angels sitting inside of the sepulcher*

Matthew 28:9 *Jesus (pbuh) let Mary Magdalene and the other Mary hold him by his feet.*

John 20:17 *Jesus (pbuh) told Mary Magdalene not to touch him.*

__Matthew 28:20__ There is no mention of Jesus' (pbuh) ascension, at all.

__Mark 16:7-19__ Jesus (pbuh) ascended to heaven, while seating at the table with his disciples, possibly in Galilee.

__Luke 24:50-51__ Jesus (pbuh) ascended to heaven in Bethany on the same day as his resurrection.

__John 21:22-25__ No mention of Jesus (pbuh) ascension, at all.

__Acts 1:3-12__ Jesus (pbuh) ascended to heaven in the Mt. Olive, forty days after his resurrection.

With the existence of so many discrepancies between the events of the supposed death of Jesus (pbuh), it is little wonder why there existed early Christian groups, like the Basilidians, who doubted that the crucifixion ever took place. Many of these examples are contradictions, but most are different versions of the same story. Some apologists prefer to marry the different versions together to get a complete story. For example, every gospel in the Bible has a different wording for the sign on the cross.

__Matthew 27:37__ And set up over his head his accusation written, THIS IS JESUS THE KING OF THE JEWS.

__Mark 15:26__ And the superscription of his accusation was written over, THE KING OF THE JEWS.

__Luke 23:38__ And a superscription also was written over him in letters of Greek, and Latin, and Hebrew, THIS IS THE KING OF THE JEWS.

__John 19:19__ And Pilate wrote a title, and put it on the cross. And the writing was JESUS OF NAZARETH THE KING OF THE JEWS.

The apologist might say the actual wording was "This is Jesus of Nazareth the King of the Jews." This would incorporate every gospel's wording, but it also declares that every gospel is incorrect, because telling part of the truth is equivalent to being disingenuous or being mistaken.

An example of a contradiction between the gospel accounts is that Jesus (pbuh) answered Pilate "never a word" (Matt. 27:14), whereas John records that "Jesus answered" three different questions of Pilate. It is rather difficult to merge Jesus (pbuh) never saying a word to Pilate and Jesus (pbuh) answering him 3 times. I have read several responses to the discrepancies in the text of the gospels and the explanations are undoubtedly done with the sole purpose of convincing other Christians that the problem is taken care of. They want to convince fellow Christians that there is no need to fret and especially no need to check out their explanation. This is because any research of the explanation given would render the explanation completely implausible. The best explanation they have is that the gospels do not tell the full story by themselves, therefore they must be interwoven together to get the full picture. So, when one gospel makes mention of an earthquake and people rising from the dead and coming out of their graves due to the death of Jesus (pbuh) and the other gospels omit these small details, it is not a big deal. We must understand the gospel writers to be only telling half-truths from their memory of an event. But how would the judge, jury and prosecutor look upon a witness, who would forgot such powerful events surrounding someone's death, especially considering that the witnesses are inspired by the Holy Spirit?

THE WITNESSES

The reason that these problems exist is apparent and completely understandable. They were not works inspired by God. They were the works of ordinary men who scholars believed were influenced by Paul's epistles, and who were vulnerable to their own biases, mistakes and memory. It is some scholars belief that the gospels of Matthew and John were actually written by Jesus' (pbuh) disciples by the same names, but these scholars are in the minority, due to the fact that the gospels are written in the third person and they are host to a plethora of mistakes and inconsistencies amongst each other as well as the other two gospels. It stands to reason that two disciples of Jesus (pbuh) would tell somewhat of the same story, but Matthew shared its commonality with Mark and Luke, both of whom were not disciples, and John is distinctive from all three.

Another reason why Matthew is not thought to be the work of a disciple is because he and Luke are accused by Bible scholars of copying their gospels from Mark and an unknown source, called the mysterious Q document. Furthermore, none of the authors of the gospels are actually known. They are assumed by tradition to be the authors of the gospels. This is why there is the words "the gospels according to Matthew," "the gospels according to Mark," etc. and not "the gospels by Matthew" and the "gospels by Mark" because none of them autographed their books. In other words, it is not an established fact but a good guess as to who the authors of these books are.

Rather strange is the fact that Jesus spoke Aramaic (Matt. 5:22, Mark 5:41, 7:34, 14:36, 15:34, John 20:16) and the people he ministered to spoke Aramaic, but the gospels are written in Greek. It is common knowledge that there is always some degree of lose in meaning of words when they are translated from one language to another. Therefore translating from Aramaic to Greek and then into other languages increases this deficiency. Not to mention that the Bible was at one time solely in the hands of the Catholic Church. It was a crime at one time to own a Bible. When we take into account all these factors, it is understandable why the gospels are filled with discrepancies. Though the witnesses to this event are anonymous, of questionable character and their testimony has possibly been copied from each other and possibly altered from its origin, we will continue on.

The reason that the witnesses and their credibility are discussed is because it is my claim that the gospels portray two different Jesus' (pbuh) at the time of his death; one willing to be killed and one that is not. One Jesus (pbuh) that has been killed on the cross and one that has not. Just as the Bible holds two different stances on the doctrine of sin, atonement and forgiveness, so, too, does it hold two different portraits of Jesus (pbuh). It is up to me to present my case and show that it is the more plausible explanation. The Christians have a more daunting task. Every Sunday morning, they present their case. But as those who believe the Bible to be the words of God, they must dismiss every facet of my case as a total misunderstanding or show how their picture of Jesus (pbuh) and my picture of Jesus (pbuh) are one.

READING THE GOSPELS WITH AN OPEN MIND

I often wonder what people might believe if they only read the gospels. Ahmed Deedat said, if you only follow the words of Jesus (pbuh), you would be a Muslim. Such a bold statement, whether true or false, calls for a re-analysis of the gospels. The words and actions of the person by whom the entire faith is based should coincide with the faith itself, but as I believe I have shown, it does not. Therefore, it is my claim that in order for anyone to read the four gospels and believe that Jesus' (pbuh) death was an inevitable event that had to occur to bring about the salvation of man, they had to have the idea before reading the books. Now, armed with the knowledge of the actual teaching of Jesus (pbuh), how does someone view the crucifixion of Jesus (pbuh)? Knowing now that he had already finished the work God gave him to do, knowing that he came to reform a portion of the Jews, knowing that forgiveness is through good deeds, helping others and repentance, knowing that he was not God, and that human sacrifice is not atonement for sin, Jesus' (pbuh) death becomes the senseless murder of a prophet of God. It is a cruel, despicable, humiliating torture of a just man for naught but to silence the truth from his mouth. When his death is thought to be for salvation, the Christians believe the ends justify the means, but this case is thrown out. Now it seems almost incumbent on God to save his prophet from such agony and vindicate Jesus (pbuh) from all those who rejected him or misunderstood him. It is saddening when the gospels suggest that Jesus (pbuh) sought death to rid himself of the disciple's lack of understanding (Matt. 17:17). Perhaps this can be chalked up as a moment of frustration, because it is crystal clear in the Bible that Jesus (pbuh) DOES NOT WANT TO DIE.

A WILLING SACRIFICE?

Despite the countless times Jesus (pbuh) is said to have referenced his own death, he did not want to die. In the gospels, Jesus (pbuh) speaks of rising from the dead after the third day of his death. He was so adamant about this happening, that it is surprising to me the extent at which Jesus (pbuh) went to postpone such an amazing event. At the "last supper," Jesus (pbuh) instructs his disciples to sell their garments and buy SWORDS. At which point, Jesus (pbuh) speaks of the events about to occur as being foretold. If the events were foretold, then the prophecy should also note that Jesus (pbuh) wished to defend himself against attacks. Yet Christians never produce such a prophecy. Nonetheless, Jesus (pbuh) did have his disciples arm themselves.

Selling your clothes for swords is an act of desperation and self-preservation. Safety has trumped all other aspects of life. One does not need swords if he is content with death. Yet the disciples sell their garments and obtain two swords, which Jesus (pbuh) says is enough. Jesus (pbuh) and his disciples go to the garden of Gethsemane to "PRAY and to WATCH" (Matt. 26:41). This is very important in understanding Jesus' (pbuh) motives. Jesus (pbuh) was already in the upper room of a house, why would he go to the Mount of Olives to a garden to pray? Couldn't he pray in the same huge place, which was large enough to accommodate 12 other people? He went to the garden of Gethsemane not only to pray but to form a resistance against those seeking to kill him, thus his disciples stood WATCH. He would have been a sitting target for an easy ambush had he stayed in the upper room of a house, when his enemies came to kill him.

When Jesus (pbuh) and the disciples arrived at the garden, Jesus (pbuh) strategically positions them as well. He had eight disciples at the gate (Matt. 26:36) and Peter the Rock and the sons of Zebedee, James and John, were his inner line of defense (Matt. 26:37, Mark 14:33). Yet Jesus' (pbuh) soul was in agony and sorrow almost to the point death (Matt. 26:38). Why? Because he wanted no part of a crucifixion. Jesus (pbuh) went further behind his inner line.

__Matthew 26:39__ And he went a little farther, and fell on his face, and prayed, saying, O my Father, if it be possible, let this cup pass from me: nevertheless not as I will, but as thou wilt.

It is abundantly clear that Jesus (pbuh) wanted nothing to do with this humiliating and excruciating punishment. Jesus (pbuh) rises from his prayers to find his disciples asleep. Upset, Jesus (pbuh) scoffs at Peter because his disciples couldn't stand WATCH for one hour (Matt. 26:40). That's correct! Jesus (pbuh) prayed to be saved from death for an entire hour. Earlier in Matthew, Jesus (pbuh) rebukes Peter, calling him satan, because Peter couldn't believe that Jesus (pbuh) would be killed (Matt. 16:16-23). Hypocritically Jesus (pbuh) is now praying to have his own prophecy of his death overturned. It is my belief that Jesus (pbuh) never made such a prophecy nor cursed his disciple in such a manner. This would explain why Jesus (pbuh) was so afraid of death.

Jesus (pbuh) also says "the flesh is weak but the spirit is willing." Christians sometimes use this phrase to explain why Jesus (pbuh) was praying so earnestly to be saved from death. The problem is Jesus (pbuh) was not speaking of his flesh and spirit, but that of the disciples. He was speaking in reference to them continuously falling to the temptation of sleep while on duty. In any case, an hour of prayer was not sufficient in Jesus' (pbuh) eyes. He proceeded to his designated prayer ground a second time. After some time, Jesus (pbuh) comes out to check on his guards and again he finds them asleep. Mark 14:41 says they fell asleep on watch three different times.

Matthew 26:44 _And he left them, and went away again, and prayed the third time, saying the SAME WORDS._

It appears that Jesus (pbuh) has given up on his disciples as a defense. He went back to God for help. Without any stretch of the imagination, it is possible that Jesus (pbuh) prayed for up to 3 hours not to be killed, over and over and over again. This may not even be considered prayer, but begging to be saved from death.

During Jesus' (pbuh) prayers, we find that an angel came from heaven and strengthened Jesus (pbuh) (Luke 22:43). Did the angel comfort him with the message that God would save him from his gruesome death or did the angel encourage him to face his imminent death? The answer to this question lies with Jesus (pbuh) on the cross, which is soon to be discussed. Nevertheless, Jesus (pbuh) continued to pray to be saved from death even after he is strengthened.

__Luke 22:44__ And being in an agony he prayed more earnestly: and his sweat was as it were great drops of blood falling down to the ground.

One might consider the famous John 3:16 and wonder does God's love spoken of in this verse included the sacrifice of a frightened man, who has guards, who sweats profusely, who is in physical pain due to his circumstances and who begs for hours to be spared. Is the killing of this innocent man an act of love?

In Mel Gibson's "Passion of Christ," satan asks Jesus (pbuh) does he believe that one man can bear the full burden of the sins of the world. This question is never, ever asked of Jesus (pbuh) by anyone in the New Testament. This is purely from Mel's imagination.

Gibson is trying to give the impression that Jesus (pbuh) was praying to God because he was uncertain that he could bear the sin of the world, when he was clearly praying to be saved him death. Christians maintain that Jesus' (pbuh) main purpose on earth was to die for the sins of mankind. I am confused as to why Jesus (pbuh) eluded death on several occasions, if this was his main purpose. Jesus (pbuh) moved about in secret to avoid death (John 7:1, 11:54) and he escaped death (John 8:58-59, 10:39). According to Jesus (pbuh), his mission was already cut short (John 16:12-13), so Jesus (pbuh) should have gone on with it. Some may suggest that he was acting in accordance with the prophecies. This raises another question, if he knew everything about his death and this was his purpose, why was he afraid to die on the cross? When death approached he resisted at every turn.

HIS CAPTURE AND SENTENCING

After his lengthy prayers, Jesus (pbuh) notices his enemies coming in his direction and he spoke to Judas, his betrayer.

Matthew 26:50 And Jesus said unto him, Friend, wherefore art thou come? Then came they, and laid hands on Jesus and took him.

Despite the endless prayers to be saved, Jesus' (pbuh) proclamation that one of his disciples would betray him, and Judas' conspicuous absence, Jesus (pbuh) seems totally unaware of Judas' motives. Calling Judas his "friend" and asking "why are you here" have been traditionally understood to be a hint of sarcasm on Jesus' (pbuh) part. But I submit to you, that it is possible that Jesus (pbuh) may not have made these bold predictions of his death and he sincerely was unaware that Judas was to betray him. I doubt that a man with the intensity and tenacity to pray for three hours is in the mood for sarcasm. However, Judas kisses Jesus (pbuh) to identify him to the armed "band of men and officers of the chief priests and Pharisees" (John 18:3). These men were described as a "great multitude," perhaps this is because Jesus (pbuh) and his disciples were taken aback by the number of men sent to arrest him. And this band of men were most likely trained Roman soldiers. Yet, Peter draws his swords and cuts off the ear of one of the captors, Malchus (John 18:10), but Jesus (pbuh) rebukes him.

Matthew 26:52 Then said Jesus unto him, Put up again thy sword into his place: for all they that take the sword shall perish with the sword.

Matthew 26:53 Thinkest thou that I cannot now pray to my Father, and he shall presently give me more than twelve legions of angels?

Matthew 26:54 But how then shall the scriptures be fulfilled, that thus it must be?

John tells a similar story of Jesus (pbuh) rebuking Peter. If you read the gospel of Matthew and John alone, there is no problem. Jesus (pbuh) doesn't condone fighting in these gospels. Jesus (pbuh) says he has the power to stop his arrest if he chose to, but he doesn't stop it to fulfill the scriptures. Jesus (pbuh) insinuates that resistance to his capture means you don't believe in his ability to stop his capture and you are going against scriptural prophecies. Here is the problem: Jesus (pbuh) told the disciples to buy swords, but only Luke records this. So when Jesus (pbuh) rebukes Peter, he is rebuking himself for lack of faith in his own power and the power of the prophecy. This gives me further reason to doubt Jesus' (pbuh) oft predictions of his death. If he did pray to be saved and have his disciples sell their clothes for swords, he probably did not say the words recorded in Matthew 26:52-54, in which he candidly speaks about his death as a scriptural fulfillment.

In Luke, Jesus (pbuh) told his disciples that two swords were enough, perhaps expecting a small band of men to attack him. Now he is facing a "GREAT MULTITUDE" and he decides to surrender. And after Jesus (pbuh) is captured, all his disciples "forsook him and fled" (Mark 14:50). Oddly enough, Mark inserts the act of an unknown man at the time of Jesus' (pbuh) arrest.

Mark 14:51 *And there followed him a certain young man, having a linen cloth cast about his naked body; and the young men laid hold on him:*

Mark 14:52 *And he left the linen cloth, and fled from them naked.*

What is the significance of this event? Mark is the only gospel to record this, but its existence is eye rising to say the least. Who was this man? Why was he following Jesus (pbuh)? Why was he only clothed with a linen cloth? Who were the "young men" who laid hold of him? And what became of this naked man? Nonetheless, Jesus (pbuh) was taken to Annas, Caiaphas, Herod Antipas and Pontius Pilate for his trial.

The chief priest, the elders and the council were in search of witnesses to Jesus' (pbuh) supposed crime of blasphemy. The gospels insist that their motive was to find false witnesses against Jesus (pbuh), but even those witnesses contradicted each other's story. When they found competent witnesses, Jesus (pbuh) does not respond to their allegations (Mark 14:56). He remains silent until the high priest asks him if he is the son of God (Mark 14:61), to which Jesus (pbuh) says "you say that I am" (Luke 22:70). This is obviously not a confession, yet the high priest, seeking anything to condemn Jesus (pbuh), pronounces his words as a blasphemous admittance of guilt (Matt. 26:65). Apparently, they will sink to any level to get rid of Jesus (pbuh), because even if he said "yes, I am" as one gospel records, the title "son of God" is not blasphemous in the Bible. The Bible is filled with men called the son of God (Gen. 6:2, Psalms 82:6, Matt. 5:9). Even God calls people his son in the Bible (2Sam. 7:14, Ex. 4:22). Therefore the outrage of the high priest was for mere show, perhaps for his audience. This is supported by the words of Jesus (pbuh) recorded in John when Jesus (pbuh) is questioned by the high priest Annas.

John 18:19 The high priest then asked Jesus of his disciples, and of his doctrine.

John 18:20 Jesus answered him, I spake openly to the world; I ever taught in the synagogue, and in the temple, whither the Jews always resort; and in secret have I said nothing.

John 18:21 Why askest thou me? ask them which heard me, what I have said unto them: behold, they know what I said.

John 18:22 And when he had thus spoken, one of the officers which stood by struck Jesus with the palm of his hand, saying, Answerest thou the high priest so?

John 18:23 Jesus answered him, If I have spoken evil, bear witness of the evil: but if well, why smitest thou me?

Jesus (pbuh) basically says that everyone knows what I teach. It is no secret. Jesus (pbuh) is aware of the fact that this is a kangaroo court and a mock trial. He has not said or done anything blasphemous. And his defense of himself is so potent that an officer tries to silence him. When Jesus (pbuh) demands to know what he has done wrong, "Annas had sent him bound unto Caiaphas the high priest" (John 18:24). It is apparent that this court has no evidence against Jesus (pbuh), and it is also apparent that Jesus (pbuh) does put up a good defense, which again implies that he was not willing to die.

After this trial, Jesus (pbuh) is sent to the Roman governor, Pontius Pilate. Because the Romans worshipped many gods, saying that Jesus (pbuh) blasphemed would not be of any great concern to Pilate. Therefore the Jews changed the charges from blasphemy to sedition, in order to have Jesus (pbuh) killed (Luke 22:67- 23:3).

Their antics did not go unnoticed by Pilate. He knew that their hatred of Jesus (pbuh) was not due to any crime, but due to "envy" (Matt. 27:18).

Luke 23:4 *Then said Pilate to the chief priests and to the people, I find no fault in this man.*

Pilate had no ground to stand on against Jesus (pbuh). Jesus (pbuh) said earlier to the Jews who came to get him in a conflict with the government to "render what is Caesar's to Caesar and render what is God's to God (Matt. 22:21)." By saying this, Jesus (pbuh) did not offended Caesar and the Roman Government nor did he offended the laws of Moses (pbuh), so he got out of the dilemma that the Jews were trying to bait him into. And Pilate asked him was he the king of the Jews, to which Jesus (pbuh) replied "my kingdom is not of this world (John 18:36)." Thus the charge of sedition could not stick.

Still with vengeance in the hearts of the chief priests, Pilate's findings only enraged Jesus' (pbuh) enemies more (Luke 23:5). Pilate discovered that Jesus (pbuh) was from the jurisdiction of Herod Antipas and he sent Jesus (pbuh) to Herod, to avoid condemning an innocent man because of the envy of ours. Jesus (pbuh) would not answer queries given by Herod, so Herod's men mocked Jesus (pbuh) and sent him back to Pilate. By the way, all of these trials are taking place early in the morning (John 18:28, Matt. 27:1). Pilate says he has "examined" Jesus (pbuh) and found no fault in him. Herod had come up with the same results (23:13-16), so Pilate says he will chastise Jesus (pbuh) and release him to appease the crowd. Of course, the chief priest and the elders were unhappy with this suggestion and they protested, thus Pilate offered another alternative.

Pilate says that it was a custom at the Passover feast to release one prisoner, so he suggested they choose between Jesus (pbuh) and a prisoner named Barabbas (John 18:39). The people chose Jesus (pbuh), despite the fact that Pilate pitted him against a man convicted of robbery (John 18:40), sedition and murder (Luke 23:25). Pilate was doing everything he could think of to have Jesus (pbuh) released. Luke says that Pilate was "willing to release Jesus (pbuh)," some translate it that he "wanted to release Jesus (pbuh)" (23:20). Pilate pleaded with the crowd three times to choose Jesus (pbuh) for release. He knew that this was a travesty of justice. Not to mention that Pilate's wife warned him to have no part in harming Jesus (pbuh) because he was a just man (Matt. 27:19). His wife said that she had suffered many things in a dream because of Jesus (pbuh). The Bible often times describes God giving revelations to people in dreams, like Abraham (pbuh) and John. It appears that God is intervening in the court process to have Jesus (pbuh) eradicated without harm. This is the message of her dream and the message she gave to her husband. In light of the priest and elder's motive, the lack of evidence against Jesus (pbuh) and his wife's warning, Pilate washed his hands of the innocent blood of Jesus (pbuh), literally (Matt. 27:24), but he released Jesus (pbuh) to the multitudes. Because Pilate released Jesus (pbuh) to his persecutors, he was not fully absolved of the crime of killing an innocent man. And his role in this event was not over.

The gospels record that Jesus (pbuh) was beaten, spit on, and mocked before his execution. In Mel Gibson's "Passion of Christ," Jesus (pbuh) is mistakenly sentenced to a flogging to death. After a very graphic and brutal beating, the soldiers beating Jesus (pbuh) are informed that he is to be crucified, not beaten to death. There is no gospel record of such a mistake in the form of execution, but I assume Mel gave Jesus (pbuh) this horrific beating to fulfill a supposed prophecy of Jesus (pbuh) in Isaiah 52:14, which says "his appearance will be marred, unlike any other man." Of course, Jews do not understand this to be speaking of Jesus (pbuh) at all, but if you subscribe to the belief of this torture of Jesus (pbuh) as Mel Gibson does, you must ignore and embellish a few things.

After seeing the brutality of the movie, I immediately went home to check up this depiction of Jesus (pbuh). I did not find it, only the mentioning of scourging Jesus (pbuh). The Roman soldiers did not have a special grudge against Jesus (pbuh). He was not given a special beating. The men of the cross next to Jesus (pbuh) most likely received the same treatment. And let's not forget Paul getting 39 lashes on 5 different occasions, being beaten with a rod on 3 occasions and being stoned once (2 Cor. 11:24-25). One would think that any of these punishments would have caused fatal wounds to Paul, but nine different times Paul eluded death (12 times, if we add the 3 times Paul was shipwreck). Also when reading the account of Jesus' (pbuh) march to his execution I found that Mel had conveniently left out some words of Jesus (pbuh). If you can recall, Jesus (pbuh) could barely stand and hold his cross in the movie. If he was beating close to the point of death, it would be hard even for Hollywood to portray a man in this state holding a cross and giving the speech recorded in the gospel of Luke.

Luke 23:28 But Jesus turning unto them said, Daughters of Jerusalem, weep not for me, but weep for yourselves, and for your children.

Luke 23:29 *For, behold, the days are coming, in the which they shall say, Blessed are the barren, and the wombs that never bare, and the paps which never gave suck.*

Luke 23:30 *Then shall they begin to say to the mountains, Fall on us; and to the hills, Cover us.*

Luke 23:31 *For if they do these things in a green tree, what shall be done in the dry?*

In Luke's gospel, Jesus (pbuh) was led directly from the trial of Pilate to the place of his execution. There was no flogging. Not only that but Luke suggests that Jesus (pbuh) did not carry the cross at all, but Simon of Cyrene was given the cross to bear as soon as Jesus (pbuh) was led away (23:26). And Jesus (pbuh) was led off with two others who were crucified (23:32), which is also absent from Gibson's film. It is more reasonable to believe that Jesus (pbuh) was not beaten and he was not carrying a cross on his back, while giving these onlookers words of comfort. How bizarre would it be to have three badly beaten men struggling up a hill with crosses on their back and one of them delivering a speech? The truth is that Jesus (pbuh) was not severely beaten as depicted in this movie. This alleged beaten was based solely on a presumption that a prophecy in the book of Isaiah pertained to Jesus (pbuh).

ON THE CROSS

Jesus (pbuh) carried his own cross in the other gospels besides Luke, until he could no longer bear it and Simon of Cyrene carried it the rest of the way. And where did this alleged crucifixion take place? The sight of the crucifixion was at the Place of the Skull, Golgotha (Matt. 27:33, John 19:17). Golgotha was "NEAR the city (of Jerusalem)" (John 19:20). Hebrews 13:12 describes Golgotha as being "OUTSIDE the city gate" of Jerusalem. Amazingly, it is Jesus (pbuh) who said that it is IMPOSSIBLE FOR A PROPHET TO BE KILLED OUTSIDE OF JERUSALEM (Luke 13:33). With this in mind, I continue.

The soldiers stripped Jesus (pbuh) naked and casts lots to determine who would keep his garments (Mark 15:24). This is a detail seldom discussed about the crucifixion. Jesus (pbuh) was absolutely naked on the cross, despite the paintings and pictures to the contrary. This makes the humiliation factor more pronounced. After someone dies, his or her waste excretes from their body. If they are naked, then you can imagine what kind of scene it would be. There is also a saddle or a horn on the cross, which is seldom depicted in illustrations of the crucifixion. This saddle is positioned halfway up the cross and it is used to support the weight of the person on the cross, otherwise their wrist or hands will be torn from their bodyweight. These details were a part of all crucifixions, yet Mel Gibson failed to incorporate them into his movie. I wonder why? It is because this kind of death is unfathomable for a prophet of God, let alone God himself. It is sensible to believe that God would deliver someone he has such an intimate relationship with from this ignominious death, even if it were simply to keep his message credible. Who would believe a man was sent by God and God had abandoned in this way? And the Jewish law echoes these sentiments.

Deuteronomy 13:5 *And that prophet, or that dreamer of dreams, shall be put to death; because he hath spoken to turn [you] away from the LORD your God, which brought you out of the land of Egypt, and redeemed you out of the house of bondage, to thrust thee out of the way which the LORD thy God commanded thee to walk in. So shalt thou put the evil away from the midst of thee.*

Deuteronomy 18:19 *But the prophet, which shall presume to speak a word in my name, which I have not commanded him to speak, or that shall speak in the name of other gods, even that prophet shall die.*

Therefore, Jesus' (pbuh) death, especially in this brutal manner, gives credence to the Jews' (pbuh) claim that he was a false prophet according to their laws, of which Jesus (pbuh) himself adhered to. On the cross of Jesus (pbuh) was a sign, which probably read "This is Jesus of Nazareth, the King of the Jews." I say probably of course because every gospel has a slightly difference inscription of the sign, so it can only be an educated guess as to what the sign actually said. John's gospel says that Pilate wrote this inscription on the sign in Hebrew, Greek and Latin. Most people assume that this sign was a mockery of Jesus (pbuh), but if you read closely you will see that Pilate wrote the sign this way as a show of contempt towards the Jews for unjustly persecuting Jesus (pbuh). The Jews asked Pilate to write, "I am the King of the Jews" to indicate that this is Jesus' (pbuh) claim and this is why he was punished. However, Pilate refused to change his inscription (John 19:19-22). By says Jesus (pbuh) was "the King of the Jews," it placed the blame on the Jewish leaders as if they should have accepted him, but instead they had their king killed. This is in fact the case because the Jewish people wanted to make Jesus (pbuh) king (John 6:15), but Jesus' (pbuh) message was not for prosperity on earth, but in heaven. The Jewish hierarchy was in opposition to Jesus (pbuh) and Pilate had appeased them enough, at this point. So he placed this sign on the cross as a smack in their faces. Now Jesus (pbuh) is nailed onto the cross.

Mark 15:34 *And at the ninth hour Jesus cried with a loud voice, saying, Eloi, Eloi, lama sabachthani? which is, being interpreted, My God, my God, why hast thou forsaken me?*

Jesus (pbuh) specifically asked God, why is he leaving him for dead? There should be no further doubt that Jesus (pbuh) did not want to be a sacrifice. In the book of Genesis, we find that God told Adam (pbuh) that he would die if he ate from a certain tree (Gen. 2:16-17), but after Adam (pbuh) ate from the tree he lived for 930 years (Gen. 5:5). Also in the story of the Prodigal, the father says that his son was DEAD, but now he is ALIVE (Luke 15:32), despite the fact that his son never actually died. The death, God spoke of was a separation from God as a result of his sins. Well Jesus (pbuh) too felt this death. Though Matthew says Jesus (pbuh) will be called Emmanuel (which he never was called) meaning "God with us," God was not with Jesus (pbuh) on the cross.

Jesus (pbuh) is perplexed that God has not delivered him from this punishment. He has prayed so earnestly that "his sweat was like drops of blood" (Luke 22:44), the angels strengthen him, yet he is being tortured. Jesus' (pbuh) proclamation that God forsook him verifies that the angel that strengthened him during his prayers assured him that he would be saved from death. Otherwise, Jesus' (pbuh) plea to God on the cross makes absolutely no sense.

__Psalms 37:28__ For Lord loves justice, and forsakes not His saints; they are preserved forever.

In light of the fact that Jesus (pbuh) was under the impression that he was to be saved from death, his words to others must be reexamined. Let's consider when Jesus (pbuh) asked for the forgiveness of his persecutors (Luke 23:34). This benevolence is not as potent as it would be if he believed that he would actually be killed. Also Jesus' (pbuh) demeanor would not be somber if he were promised salvation from the cross.

Matthew and Mark record Jesus (pbuh) asking why God has forsaken him and then Jesus (pbuh) gives up his ghost. Without these words to

God, John too paints a gloomy picture of Jesus (pbuh) on the cross. However, Luke depicts Jesus (pbuh) promising salvation to someone else while he himself is in a tumultuous situation. If you are at the point of death and you believe that God has left you out to dry, why would you bless someone else? From "My God, my God, why hast thou forsaken me?" to "Verily I say unto thee, Today shalt thou be with me in paradise" is a huge jump. What caused this transition? The book of Hebrews gives us the answer to this question.

Hebrews 5:7 *Who in the days of his flesh, when he (Jesus) had offered up prayers and supplications with strong crying and tears unto him that was able to save him from death, and was heard in that he feared*

The Biblical connotation for "God heard your prayers" is that God heard AND ANSWERED your prayers, just as it was the case in the story of the birth of Ishmael (pbuh) in the book of Genesis. God heard the prayers of Abraham (pbuh) and Hagar and granted them a son named Ishmael (pbuh) which literally means "God hears." Therefore when Jesus (pbuh) prayed to be saved and God HEARD his prayer, he granted him his wish AND SAVED JESUS (pbuh) from death according to the book of Hebrews. That is why his attitude changed so dramatically. It appears that the gospels left out a detail or two in their biographies, as John admits (John 21:25), in which Jesus (pbuh) is reassured that he will be saved. So when he said "Father, into thy hands I commend my spirit" he is reaffirming his faith in God's power to save him. And his "giving up the ghost" is merely a façade which the gospel writer's themselves fell victim to. They are the ones who suggest that Jesus (pbuh) gave up the ghost. The closest thing to this from the lips of Jesus (pbuh) is when he says "It is finished" (John 19:30) in a gospel which has Jesus (pbuh) already "finished" (John 17:4).

Some of the last words of Jesus (pbuh) are very intriguing. When he (pbuh) cries out "My God, My God, why have you forsaken me?" he is speaking in reference to the prophecy spoke of in the book of Psalms. Close analysis of this chapter of Psalms reveals startling facts.

Psalms 22:1 My God, my God, why have you forsaken me? Why are you so far from saving me, so far from my cries of anguish?
Psalms 22:2 My God, I cry out by day, but you do not answer, by night, but I find no rest.

Psalms 22:7 All who see me mock me; they hurl insults, shaking their heads.
Psalms 22:8 "He trusts in the LORD," they say, "let the LORD rescue him. Let him deliver him, since he delights in him."

Psalms 22:14 I am poured out like water, and all my bones are out of joint. My heart has turned to wax; it has melted within me.
Psalms 22:15 My mouth is dried up like a potsherd, and my tongue sticks to the roof of my mouth; you lay me in the dust of death.

Psalms 22:16 Dogs surround me, a pack of villains encircles me; they pierce my hands and my feet.
Psalms 22:17 All my bones are on display; people stare and gloat over me.
Psalms 22:18 They divide my clothes among them and cast lots for my garment.

Psalms 22:19 But you, LORD, do not be far from me. You are my strength; come quickly to help me.
Psalms 22:20 Deliver me from the sword, my precious life from the power of the dogs.
Psalms 22:21 Rescue me from the mouth of the lions; save me from the horns of the wild oxen.

This chapter of Psalms captures the scene of the crucifixion almost explicitly. Yet it goes further to demonstrate that Jesus (pbuh) continues to seek deliverance from this ignoble death. And even more astounding is that the prophecy which Jesus (pbuh) quotes is actually one in which God actually intervenes and rescues his pleading servant. The chapter ends as praise to God for his deliverance.

Psalms 22:31 He has done it!

If Jesus (pbuh) quoted this Psalm, he must have known that the Psalm's prophecy ends in his rescue. Also the last words of Jesus (pbuh) in John's Gospel was "It is finished!" "Possibly the Fourth Gospel unrealising makes Jesus say, 'It is finished,' when in fact he had come to the last words of Psalms 22:32: 'He has done it.'" (Hugh Schonfield, "The Passover Plot") The words "done and "finish" are synonymous, thus it is quite possible that the phrases, "It is done" and "He has done it" were mistakenly or purposely interchanged. Since Jesus (pbuh) is aware that God will inevitably rescue him, it makes sense that he transforms from a deserted and desperate man to a man of solace, trusting in God, as he says in Luke, "Father in your hands I commend my spirit."

And there is more evidence to show that Jesus' (pbuh) prayers were answered and he was not killed. The synoptic gospels tell us that Jesus (pbuh) was on the cross at about the sixth hour or 12 o'clock and he died after the ninth hour or 3 o'clock (Matt. 27:45, Mark 15:33, Luke 23:44-45). John tells us, that Jesus (pbuh) was on the cross but he was to be taken down because the Sabbath was approaching (John 19:31). It was a sacrilege to have someone hanging on a cross on the Sabbath day, thus Jesus (pbuh) was taken down from the cross. Unlike western society, the Jews consider a day starting at night. There is nighttime then daytime, when our view of a day is daytime and nighttime. When the moon is spotted, a new day begins in their system. The Sabbath starts around 6 o'clock on Friday. They arrested Jesus (pbuh) Thursday night, and tried him several times in the morning, mocked and flogged him, then put him on a cross.

Jesus (pbuh) was only on the cross for three or maybe four hours before he was to be taken down by 6 o'clock. Because there is to be no work done on the Sabbath, the preparation for his burial must be included in the time before 6 o'clock, as well. How convenient that Jesus (pbuh) died just in time! The problem is crucifixion is a slow process. Its sole purpose is pain and humiliation for an extended amount of time until one dies of asphyxiation. There have been cases of people doing mock crucifixions as an honor to Jesus (pbuh), in which they endure the very same method of crucifixion as Jesus (pbuh) is said to have endured and they have stayed on the cross for two and three days, to later walk away. This should give pause to anyone who thinks he died in a few hours on the cross. The fact that Jesus (pbuh) was only on the cross for a few hours necessitates the brutal beating that "The Passion of the Christ" created.

Another reason to doubt Jesus' (pbuh) death was that Pilate could not believe that Jesus (pbuh) died in such a short time. As someone who sentenced people to crucifixion on a regular basis, Pilate knew this was practically impossible (Mark 15:44). Add to this the fact that Jesus' (pbuh) two cross mates were still alive (John 19:31-33). It is no doubt that Jesus (pbuh), as a man knowledgeable about his faith, knew that he must be taken down before the Sabbath, thus he thought it wise to pretend to be dead, in order to escape. The alternative is to believe that a Prophet of God who was born miraculously, who raised people from the dead, who walked on water, who cured leprosy, blindness and demon-possessed people, was easily killed in three hours by a process geared to take days to complete.

JESUS (pbuh) TAKEN OFF OF THE CROSS

Because those on the cross must be taken down before the Sabbath and because crucifixion was to be a slow lingering death, there would arise occasions in which the criminal would still be ALIVE when he was taken down. When this happened the prisoner's legs were broken. Both the men with Jesus (pbuh) on the cross had their legs broken, but Jesus (pbuh) did not have his legs broken (John 19:32-33) because the soldiers SAW that Jesus (pbuh) was dead already. There have been innumerous cases of people escaping death by pretending to be dead. The victim is injured and the criminal perceives them to be dead. Even professional doctors have pronounced their patients to be deceased, when in fact they are actually ALIVE. One of the soldiers speared Jesus (pbuh) in his side to ensure that Jesus (pbuh) had died. Perhaps he did not take the first soldier's observation as sufficient. And immediately blood and water came out of the wound (John 19:34). Had Jesus (pbuh) been dead, his blood would have begun to clot. This blood coming "forthwith" is another testament that Jesus (pbuh) was still ALIVE.

"Forthwith" means that it came out immediately. The blood and water were not slowly leaking or oozing out, as would have been the case if the person were dead already. "The reported emission of blood shows at least that life was still in him." (Hugh Schonfield, "The Passover Plot") John's gospel then speaks of the prophecy in which it says that Jesus' (pbuh) bones will not be broken (19:36). Let us have a look at that prophecy.

Psalms 34:20 *Many are the ills of the righteous, but Lord delivereth him out of them all.*

Psalms 34:21 *He keepeth all his bones; not one of them is broken.*

If this prophecy is about Jesus (pbuh), then God WILL DELIVER him from ALL difficulties, including the CRUCIFIXION. This is another confirmation that God HEARD the prayers of Jesus (pbuh) to be saved.

When Jesus (pbuh) is said to have died, a great phenomenon occurred. At once, the curtains of the temple of Jerusalem were split, there was an earthquake, graves of the dead were opened, saints were resurrected from the dead and they walked the streets, and there was an eclipse of the sun for 3 hours (Luke 23:44-45). There has never been a sequence of such extraordinary events recorded in history. Some may consider this to be a personification of God's anger. But there is no record of anyone being harmed in all this. It was a diversion from Jesus' (pbuh) condition and his chance to escape from death.

When Pilate is given news of Jesus' (pbuh) death, he marvels (Mark 15:44), he wants to know how long has Jesus (pbuh) been dead? The interesting thing is that he asks the centurion this question. This is the centurion who NOW believes Jesus (pbuh) to be the son of God and a righteous man (Mark 15:39, Luke 23:47). The centurion gave him an answer, which is not recorded, and Pilate gave Jesus' (pbuh) body over to Joseph, a secret disciple of Jesus (pbuh) (John 19:38). We have established that Pilate wanted no part of Jesus' (pbuh) death. In fact, he was very AFRAID to take any part in it (John 19:8). So we have two believers (Joseph and the centurion) and a Jesus' (pbuh) sympathizer (Pilate), who held Jesus' (pbuh) fate. Could it not be that the centurion informed Pilate that Jesus (pbuh) was alive and Pilate now found a way to relieve himself of any guilt and wrongdoing? If Jesus (pbuh) were ALIVE, would Pilate not help to keep him alive, in light of everything he knew?

"It is by no means a novel theory that Jesus was not dead when taken from the cross, and some will have it that he subsequently recovered... However, we have to imagine very little since Mark and John agree on what is essential to the requirements of the situation. We have only to allow that in this as in other instances Jesus made private arrangements with someone he could trust, who would be in a position to accomplish his design. This person is identified to us in the Gospels as Joseph of Arimathea" (Hugh Schonfield, "The Passover Plot")

Interestingly enough, it is Joseph who took Jesus (pbuh) off of the cross (Luke 23:53). The gospels refer to Jesus (pbuh) as "it." The authors are still under the assumption that Jesus (pbuh) is dead and Joseph is taking a dead body down, but Joseph asks for the body (soma) of Jesus (pbuh), not his corpse (ptoma). (Fortunately for my sake, the writers of gospel can never be considered infallible due to their numerous errors, omissions and contradicts, some of which have been cited earlier. The presence of these discrepancies allows me to read the gospels without taking every word as the "gospel truth.") Now Joseph, the "secret" disciple of Jesus (pbuh) (John 19:38), and Nicodemus, a Pharisees and ruler of the Jews (John 3:1), took Jesus (pbuh) away from the cross. Nicodemus is spoken of briefly in the gospel of John, only. Because he is a Pharisee, it is clear that he is acting in secret as Joseph is, because Pharisees were some of Jesus' (pbuh) biggest detractors. We must ask ourselves, what is the motive for having secret disciples? When you have someone as a secret supporter, you conceal their identity for a greater purpose. It seems that their grand purpose is at hand.

Joseph and Nicodemus prepared Jesus (pbuh) for burial, wrapping him in linen cloth with spices weighing 100 pounds (John 19:39-40). Joseph was a counselor and a rich man. He had his own land, where he laid Jesus (pbuh) in a brand new sepulcher. This sepulcher Joseph, himself, had hewn out of rock (Matt. 27:60). Jesus (pbuh) was not put in a grave. A sepulcher is a tomb or room in which the dead are placed. Sepulchers would allow for breathing and movement, both of which would be needed for someone who is ALIVE. Obviously, Joseph had the sepulcher built long before Jesus (pbuh) was arrested, so he had planned and prepared this place for Jesus (pbuh).

Meanwhile, the chief priest and the Pharisees recalled Jesus (pbuh) saying he would rise on the third day after his death. They feared that the disciples would steal Jesus (pbuh) away and say that he had risen. So the chief priest and the Pharisees go to the sepulcher with a guard

(Pilate affords them one guard to stand post at the tomb. Strangely the next day, the day after the Sabbath, there is more than one guard at the tomb Matt.28:4) thinking that their "last error shall be worse than the first" (Matt. 27:64). The last error they speak of is allowing his secret disciples to put him in a sepulcher. So what was the first error? Probably, allowing Joseph to take Jesus (pbuh) off of the cross without their verification of his death. Since the gospels do not explain these errors, it is left to speculation. Now in desperation, they go to the sepulcher. On the Sabbath day, they seal the tomb closed with a stone (Matt. 27:62-66). This is despite the fact that the gospel of Matthew has stated that Joseph ALREADY rolled the stone to the door (Matt. 27:60). Apparently, when Joseph rolled the stone, he left an opening. I wonder why? Also remember that they were observing the Sabbath but they broke the Sabbath to CORRECT their first mistake. This mistake had to be extremely important to them.

At the end of the Sabbath, there was another earthquake. This earthquake was due to an angel descending to earth from heaven (Matt. 28:2). This would explain the earlier earthquake. Perhaps an angel came down after Jesus (pbuh) supposed death and caused that earthquake, as well. This would explain how there were TWO angels in the tomb of Jesus (pbuh) in Luke and John's gospel when Matthew and Mark speak of only one angel. When did the other angel come down and for what reason? Surely when he came he also caused an earthquake, which would be the earthquake that occurred when Jesus (pbuh) was said to have given up the ghost. If he gave up his ghost to the angel, why was the angel still on earth? No, the angel strengthened and protected Jesus (pbuh).

Another point to ponder is that the centurion and those with him believed in Jesus (pbuh) because as they were watching Jesus (pbuh). They saw the earthquake "and those things that were done" (Matt. 27:54). What were those things done? It could not have simply been the earthquake and the veil being torn because all the witnesses surely saw this. Because the centurion was the one able to say how long Jesus (pbuh) was dead, it is clear that he was the closest person to Jesus (pbuh). Thus he would have witnessed the angel coming to Jesus (pbuh) and aiding him. This angel's descent to earth and its aiding of Jesus (pbuh) were "those things done" which commanded the centurion's conversion. The gospel of Mark disagrees with Matthew and Luke when they say "those things done" changed the centurion. Mark suggests that Jesus' (pbuh) death converted the centurion which makes absolutely no sense in my mind. If death caused his conversion, then every person that the centurion saw crucified was an innocent and righteous son of God as he claimed Jesus (pbuh) was (Luke 23:47, Mark 15:39).

AT THE TOMB

The angel, who came on the Sabbath, came to open the tomb, which the guards had closed. And they told those who entered that Jesus (pbuh) was not there (Matt. 28:2-7). Mary Magdalene and Mary the mother of James and Salome and perhaps others had witnessed everything that happened from the cross (Matt. 27:55-56, John 19:25), to Joseph and Nicodemus preparing the burial (Luke 23:55) and the angels inside the tomb (Luke 24:5). They were eyewitness to all these events. If Jesus (pbuh) were alive, they would have known it. Luke says the women saw where and more importantly HOW Jesus (pbuh) was laid. This detail is important because they came with spices to place around Jesus (pbuh), when they had ALREADY KNOWN that Joseph and Nicodemus put 100 pounds of spices around him. The woman came with the spices as a cover for their true motives, to find a living Jesus (pbuh).

John's gospel speaks of Mary Magdalene going by herself to the tomb of Jesus (pbuh). Interestingly enough, Mary's terminology when speaking of Jesus (pbuh) is dissimilar to that of the gospel writers. The writers, presuming Jesus (pbuh) to be dead, speak of him as "it" meaning a dead body, whereas Mary says "him" or "the Lord" giving the impression that she believes him to be ALIVE (John 20:2). When she arrives at the tomb and it is empty, she assumes that someone has taken "him" not "it" and "laid" not "buried" him somewhere. Mary is telling this to Peter and some other disciple who is nameless. They go to the sepulcher and Peter notices that the linen clothes were unwound, and the shroud from Jesus' (pbuh) face was removed (John 20:5-7). Christians assert that this is when Jesus was resurrected from the dead. At this point I would like to ask, what is the nature of a resurrected being? It is universally accepted that when you are raised from the dead, you are a spiritual being. You are immortal. And if one has any doubt about this fact, let us consult Jesus (pbuh) for the answer?

Luke 20:35 *But they which shall be accounted worthy to obtain that world, and the resurrection from the dead, neither marry, nor are given in marriage:*

Luke 20:36 *Neither can they die any more: for they are equal unto the angels; and are the children of God, being the children of the resurrection.*

If Jesus was a resurrected immortal spiritual being, why does he need two good legs, the door left open by Joseph, an angel to open the sepulcher after the guard sealed it, his linen unwrapped and his shroud taken off? None of this is necessary unless Jesus (pbuh) was a mortal human being. The EMPTY TOMB, itself, is clear evidence that he is mortal. Where were his bones? They were inside of him, walking around. Spirits don't have bones. They don't need bones. Where was his corpse? It was nowhere to be found because he was ALIVE. These things are right in our faces and yet it is difficult to see.

Matthew 13:13 _seeing, they see not_

IN DISGUISE

When the guards saw the angel descend from heaven, they were terrified almost to the point of death (Matt. 28:4). When the two Marys left the angels, the guards told the chief priest and the elders what had happened. The elders bribed the soldier to say that the disciples had stolen Jesus (pbuh) away. Apparently the soldiers told the elders and the priest that Jesus (pbuh) was no longer in the tomb, which means they would seek to have Jesus (pbuh) killed again. The two Marys, knowing this, were afraid and said nothing of it to anyone but the disciples (Mark 16:8). Why were they afraid to tell anyone about Jesus (pbuh) if he was truly resurrected? He could only be harmed if he were human. And Jesus (pbuh) knew full well the danger he faced.

At this point, Mary Magdalene is in distress. She wept as she looking in the sepulcher, believing the Jews had foiled their rescue plan. But as she spoke with the angels, "she turned herself back, and saw Jesus (pbuh) standing, and knew not that it was Jesus" (John 20:14-17). And Jesus (pbuh) asked her why is she crying and who is she looking for? She still doesn't recognize his face or his voice. Mary asked him where has he taking Jesus (pbuh) so she can "take him away." What would she want with a dead body and how will she carry it herself?

After three days, a dead person would be stiff as a log and its dead weight combined with 100 pounds of spices would be practically impossible for one person to "take away." It's clear that Mary is looking for a live physical Jesus (pbuh). But he is right in front of her, so why does she not recognize him? The reason Mary does not recognize Jesus (pbuh) is because he is in disguise as a gardener. John's gospel says "she supposed he was the gardener" (John 20:15). As Ahmed Deedat once asked, "Do resurrect bodies look like gardeners?" No, if I suppose you are a mail man, it is most likely because you are dressed as a mail man. As one of my most intimate friends, who I am already looking for and looking at, you must be in disguise for me to see you and speak with you and then confuse you with the mailman. Now, Jesus (pbuh) decided to unmask himself and he called her name in a manner in which she recognized. Mary, elated, wished to embrace Jesus (pbuh).

John 20:17 _Jesus saith unto her, Touch me not; for I am not yet ascended to my Father_

Jesus (pbuh) perhaps in pain from his injuries does not want Mary to touch him. This has to be the case, considering that Jesus (pbuh) will soon after allow his other disciples to touch him. Also, it is apparent to Mary that Jesus (pbuh) has not ascended to his Father, he is right in front of her, so what is he trying to convey to Mary? He is saying to Mary, I am not dead yet. I am not resurrected. I am ALIVE and it will hurt if you touch me.

Jesus (pbuh) tells Mary that he is ALIVE (John 20:17)

Mary told the disciples that he is ALIVE (Mark 16:11)

Angels say he is ALIVE (Luke 24:5)

Angels again said he is ALIVE (Luke 24:23)

I am often puzzled when I pass by a bulletin of a church was reads "Jesus (pbuh) is ALIVE." I wonder if anyone ever considered the tremendous difference between someone who is ALIVE and someone who is RESURRECTED. When you assert that someone is resurrected, you are saying that they were dead but they are raised from death as a spiritual being. If you say that someone is ALIVE, this means that they were PRESUMED to be dead, but they are not dead. Jesus (pbuh), the angels and Mary all confess that Jesus (pbuh) was ALIVE. The greatest Christian evangelist of all times, Paul also attests to this fact. In the book of Acts, Paul is arguing about a man called Jesus (pbuh). They said that Jesus (pbuh) was dead. But Paul says that he is "ALIVE" (Acts 25:19).

Jesus' (pbuh) testimony alone should suffice, but the story doesn't end there. There is even more evidence that Jesus (pbuh) was in disguise. After Mary recognized Jesus (pbuh) in disguise, Mark tells us that Jesus (pbuh) "appeared in another form unto two of (the disciples)." Without the description of a gardener in John, it would be left to our imagination what is meant by "another form," because the gospels speak of Jesus (pbuh) appearing seemingly out of nowhere to his disciples and leaving without a trace. With John's gospel in mind, we can see that Jesus (pbuh) was in another disguise when he met the two disciples. Without the understanding that Jesus (pbuh) is a mortal man, thus still vulnerable to death, some assume he is a ghost slipping in and out of keyholes. But he is a man in hiding. When he meets the two disciples on the road to a village called Emmaus, they thought him to be a stranger in Jerusalem, because Jesus (pbuh) acted as if he had not heard of himself. So they told Jesus (pbuh) about himself and Jesus (pbuh) began to teach them about scripture. They invited him into their home. And the manner in which Jesus (pbuh) broke and blessed the bread made them aware of who he was. And as soon as they recognized him, he left (Luke 24:13-31). How could his own disciples not know who he was unless he was in disguise? On several occasions Jesus (pbuh) escaped death while even in the grasp of his enemies.

John 10:39 *Again they tried to seize him, but he escaped their grasp.*

__John 8:59__ At this, they picked up stones to stone him, but Jesus hid himself, slipping away from the temple grounds.

__Luke 4:29-30__ They got up, drove him out of the town, and took him to the brow of the hill on which the town was built, in order to throw him off the cliff. But he walked right through the crowd and went on his way.

How is it possible that a great teacher and miracle worker could have great multitudes following him, some believers and some detractors, and he continuous slip through the cracks? Could not a miracle worker transform his image? Of course, he could. The Synoptic Gospels record his transfiguration. (Matt. 17:1-9, Mark 9:2-8, Luke 9:28-36).   Jesus (pbuh) is in the presence of his enemies (on one occasions, he is at the edge of a cliff), speaking with them and "he walked right through the crowd." It is clear that Jesus (pbuh) disguised or camouflaged himself in these dire circumstances.

PHYSICAL OR SPIRITUAL

The fact that Jesus (pbuh) was a mortal should be laid to rest with his display to his eleven disciples. He waited until they were all together to completely confirm that he was ALIVE.

__Luke 24:36__ And as they thus spake, Jesus himself stood in the midst of them, and saith unto them, Peace be unto you.

Luke 24:37 *But they were terrified and affrighted, and supposed that they had seen a spirit.*

Luke 24:38 *And he said unto them, Why are ye troubled? and why do thoughts arise in your hearts?*

Luke 24:39 *Behold my hands and my feet, that it is I myself: handle me, and see; for a spirit hath not flesh and bones, as ye see me have.*

Luke 24:40 *And when he had thus spoken, he shewed them his hands and his feet.*

Luke 24:41 *And while they yet believed not for joy, and wondered, he said unto them, Have ye here any meat?*

Luke 24:42 *And they gave him a piece of a broiled fish, and of a honeycomb.*

Luke 24:43 *And he took it, and did eat before them.*

In no uncertain terms, Jesus (pbuh) said that he is the same person you have known, slept, ate and traveled with. What then were the disciples thinking? Why were they afraid? Mary had told them that Jesus (pbuh) was ALIVE, but they didn't believe her (Mark 16:11). They thought he was dead because they "all forsook him and fled" when he was arrested. Only an unnamed disciple (John 19:26) and possibly Peter witnessed anything further (John 19:26). But they too were not present throughout the supposed death and burial of Jesus (pbuh). At one point, John's gospel has the unnamed disciple, Jesus' mother Mary, Mary the wife of Cleophas, and Mary Magdalene standing next to the cross (19:25-28). But at the time of Jesus' (pbuh) supposed death, the only witnesses to him "giving up the ghost" were the centurion, the three Marys and many other women. And all these women looked on from afar (Mark 15:39-41). It seems that the witnesses were sent away from Jesus (pbuh). And it is clear that none of the male disciples of Jesus (pbuh) witnessed the events as they unfolded and none of them saw him "give up the ghost."

Remember that Mary was not afraid when she recognized Jesus (pbuh), because she was an eyewitness to everything. But when the disciples saw Jesus (pbuh), they were "terrified and affrighted." They thought they were seeing a ghost, because Jesus (pbuh) had told them, when you are resurrected you are like an angel (Luke 20:36). But Jesus (pbuh) now assures them that he is not resurrected, but ALIVE, when he shows them his hands and feet.

As the disciples began to understand that Jesus (pbuh) escaped death, they became excited and they "WONDERED." What did they wonder? The gospel is again inconspicuously silent about what they wondered. They were probably wondering, how he escaped imminent death and how was he continuing to do so? Jesus (pbuh) perhaps hungry from all he has endured asked for food and he ate "fish and a honeycomb before them." He is still confirming his mortality. What need does a spirit have for earthly nutrients? And what point does he prove by eating it? There is no need and no point to an angelic resurrected being eating food. He can only be showing them that he is ALIVE, and not resurrected.

Remember the disciples had also mistaken Jesus (pbuh) for a spirit when he was walking on water, but he assured them that he was the same physical Jesus (pbuh) that they knew him to be there also (Matt. 14:26-27). In both cases their mistaken presumptions of Jesus' (pbuh) nature were the same and the actuality of his nature was the same, as well. He was a mortal man.

DOUBTING THOMAS

John suggests that the disciple named Thomas was not with the eleven disciples, when Jesus (pbuh) showed them his hands and feet. Despite the other disciples' testimony, Thomas said he would not believe unless he can actually put his fingers on the wounds of Jesus (pbuh). Jesus (pbuh) came to Thomas EIGHT days later and he allowed Thomas to feel his wounds in his hands and side and finally Thomas believed (John 20:24-29). What did Thomas now believe? Did he believe that a resurrected body has wounds? No, he now believed that Jesus (pbuh) was ALIVE as his disciples had witnessed and told him. What is important to note is that Jesus (pbuh) asks Mary not to touch him, but 8 days later he allowed Thomas to touch him. Why the change of heart? He is still not "ascended to (his) Father." Obviously, as time progresses your body heals and 8 days later the pain had subsided enough for Jesus (pbuh) to be touched.

We must also notice that Jesus (pbuh) is easily recognized by the disciples when he is inside (John 20:19, 26), but when he meets his disciples outside he can't be recognized. Even after he proves to his disciple that he was not resurrected, Jesus (pbuh) is outside again and he is unrecognizable as they are fishing and he is speaking directly to them from the shore (John 21:1, 4, 12). Jesus (pbuh) is in disguise. Is there any other plausible explanation to this sequence of events? I would love to hear the alternative to my view. I propose that if someone is given the four biographies of Jesus (pbuh) only, without any commentary or discussion, that many readers would conclude that Jesus (pbuh) never died on the cross, at all.

THE RESURRECTION

In short, if there is no crucifixion then there is no resurrection. The gospels record Jesus (pbuh) saying many times that he will be raised on the third day. Often times, Jesus (pbuh) said I will be killed and raised on the third day. Since it has been shown that he was not killed, I can boldly state that this is a false prophecy. This is not the only false prophecy attributed to Jesus (pbuh). He had on several occasions said that "the kingdom of God" and the end of the world were coming before his disciples and his generation died (Matt. 24:34, Mark 9:1, Luke 9:27, John 21:22). But this did not take place. If one prophecy is untrue then the others are susceptible to criticism and skepticism.

The gospel of Mark does not contain the resurrection of Jesus (pbuh), AT ALL in its earliest manuscripts. If you notice in your Bible, there is often a commentary which will explain this fact. The ending we have now is a later addition to Mark. The chapter abruptly ends when Mary finds the empty tomb in 16:8. There are at least nine alternate endings given to this gospel, but none of them are to be found in the earliest known manuscripts. These are all later additions to Mark's ending. Thus the choice of the one we have today is someone's best guess as to the ending, when the evidence suggests that all nine endings are fictitious. Mark as the earliest gospel writer, allowed his successors, Matthew, Luke and John, the opportunity to copy his work and fill in the blanks that he left.

What does resurrection mean? It is the act of rising from the dead or returning to life. In the manner in which Jesus used the words for himself, he must have meant raised from the dead or grave and not returning to life. His disciples themselves were confused by Jesus' (pbuh) words "raised on the 3rd day", but they were too afraid to ask him what he meant by this (Mark 9:10, 31-32). And they still had not received clarification as to what Jesus meant even up to his death (John 20:9). So when they heard Jesus (pbuh) had died, they took his appearances afterwards to be someone returning as a spirit, when Jesus (pbuh) meant he will be raised out of his grave or entombment ALIVE. It is Jesus (pbuh) who said that corn must DIE in order to bring forth fruit (John 12:23-24), but he did not literally mean "death" but he meant that the corn must be put into the ground. If you read these verses carefully, you will notice that Jesus (pbuh) is using the corn as a metaphor for himself, thus he is using death figuratively, not literally. This reference is also right after the raising of Lazarus. How does Jesus' (pbuh) figurative death and the raising of Lazarus correlate? We shall see.

There are three rather peculiar cases of people raised from the dead in the gospels, the daughter of the ruler of the synagogue (Mark 5:22-42), Lazarus (John 11:1-44) and the saints that came out of their graves (Matt. 27:51-53). All of them are described as sleeping. And when Jesus (pbuh) raised them up, they were physical beings. The saints went into the city and appeared to many people. The little girl went with her family and they never told of the events that took place. And Lazarus ate food and was susceptible to death (John 12:2, 10). Luke adds another story of someone raised from the dead. Jesus (pbuh) raised a widow's son. Though he is not said to be asleep, when he is revived, he too is a physical being (7:11-15). Yet Jesus (pbuh) said of the resurrected being, "neither can they die any more: for they are equal unto the angels" (Luke 20:36). After their death, all these people had the same human nature as Jesus (pbuh) did. So how can we reconcile Jesus' (pbuh) words about resurrected beings and the fact that Jesus (pbuh) and those that he raised from the dead were still mortal? The answer is that they were not actually resurrected by resuscitated, thus they are referred to as being asleep. Resuscitation is the restoration of consciousness or life functions after APPARENT death, not actual death. There have been cases of people about to be placed in a coffin and they wake up. Are they resurrected beings? No, they are resuscitated. They regain consciousness.

John's gospel is the only gospel which speaks of the rise of Lazarus. Perhaps to drawn a parallel, he mentions the napkin or shroud and the unwrapped cloths of both Lazarus and Jesus (pbuh). Jesus (pbuh) instructed the crowd to help Lazarus out of the strips of cloth in which he was wrapped from head to toe (John 11: 44). Interestingly, we find that Jesus' (pbuh) cloths were also taken off after his supposed death (John 20:6-7). Not only was Jesus (pbuh) unwrapped, but the cloths that wrapped his body were separated from the cloth for his head (John

20:6-7). And this head cloth was also "rolled up," which probably means that it was never placed on his face at all, especially since he was ALIVE.

"If we discard the charge that the body of Jesus was removed in order to claim that he had risen from the dead..., we are left with the perfectly natural and fully justifiable reason that Jesus was taken from the tomb at the first possible opportunity for the entirely legitimate purpose of reviving him." (Hugh Schonfield, "The Passover Plot")

The historian Flavius Josephus related a story eerily similar to that of the depiction of Jesus (pbuh) in the gospels. Josephus had 3 friends who were being crucified, so he asked the Roman general Titus to have them taken down ALIVE. Two of them later died from their injuries and one of them recovered.

Some apologists suggest that Jesus (pbuh) was given a special physical resurrected body, which was specifically for him. They cite the fact that the disciples thought Jesus (pbuh) was a spirit as proof of this claim. They mean to say that Jesus (pbuh) was a spiritual being, with a physical body. However, they forget that the disciples also feared him and mistook Jesus (pbuh) for a spirit when they saw him walking on water (Matt. 14:26). Was he resurrected at that time as well? This claim is nothing but conjecture used in an effort to explain away the actions Jesus (pbuh) took to prove that he was ALIVE. Jesus (pbuh) specifically told them that he was not a spirit, but the same physical body that they knew him to be (Luke 24:39). And at least 4 other people shared his "special resurrected body." The girl, Lazarus and the saints.

JESUS' (pbuh) PROPHECIES

Christians claim that there are hundreds of prophecies and events that point to the crucifixion of Jesus (pbuh). The most popular one may be the "suffering servant" described in Isaiah chapter 52 and 53. These chapters are where the idea that Jesus (pbuh) being brutally beating comes from. But even if this prophecy is in reference to Jesus (pbuh) (Jews maintain it is a metaphor for Israel), the prophecy was not fulfilled. I find it to be implausible for this to be a prophecy concerning Jesus (pbuh), mainly because it speaks of someone "lead to the slaughter like a lamb; he opened not his mouth" (Isa. 53:7). Though Jesus (pbuh) was quiet on occasion during his trial, it would be quite difficult for Jesus (pbuh) to respond to questions, as the gospels say that he did, with his mouth closed (Matt. 26:24, 27:11, Luke 23:28-3, John 18:20-21, 23, 37). Therefore this prophecy does not refer to Jesus (pbuh) or it is a false prophecy.

Did Jesus (pbuh) give any prophecy about his death? Of course, he did say that he will died and be raise again, but it must be taken as a separation from God and not actual death for his words to be true. On one occasion, Jesus (pbuh) was asked by the Jews to give them a sign in order for them to believe him, yet the gospels are at odds over what Jesus (pbuh) said in response. Matthew records the scribes and Pharisees asking Jesus (pbuh) for a sign.

Matthew 12:39 *But he answered and said unto them, An evil and adulterous generation seeketh after a sign; and there shall no sign be given to it, but the sign of the prophet Jonas:*

Matthew 12:40 *For as Jonas was three days and three nights in the whale's belly; so shall the Son of man be three days and three nights in the heart of the earth.*

Later on in Matthew, the Pharisees and the Sadducees came to Jesus (pbuh) with the same request and Jesus (pbuh) rebukes them as well, and he says they will get no sign but the sign of Jonah (pbuh) (16:1-3). However there is no mention of "three days and three nights." In the gospel of Mark, we find only one instance in which Jesus (pbuh) is asked for a sign. However, in Mark, Jesus (pbuh) says to the Pharisees only, they will get no sign at all (8:11-12). So we turn our attention to Luke for correction, since he is supposed to have written the most accurate versions of Jesus' (pbuh) life. We find that Luke does not specify who Jesus (pbuh) was addressing this prophecy to. He only describes the people seeking a sign as "others." In Luke, Jesus (pbuh) speaks of the sign of Jonah (pbuh) again with no mention of the "three days and three nights" (11:16, 11:29). Not surprisingly, John gives us another alternative.

John 2:18 Then answered the Jews and said unto him, What sign shewest thou unto us, seeing that thou doest these things?

John 2:19 Jesus answered and said unto them, Destroy this temple, and in three days I will raise it up.

John 2:20 Then said the Jews, Forty and six years was this temple in building, and wilt thou rear it up in three days?

John 2:21 But he spake of the temple of his body.

The significance of John's account is that the false witnesses in Jesus' trial accused Jesus (pbuh) of this offense (Matt. 26:61, Mark 14:58). When reading the first two gospels (Luke says nothing on the subject), it appears that the trial witnesses have totally concocted a story about Jesus (pbuh) saying destroy the temple and he will raise it in three days, because the synoptic gospels never mention Jesus (pbuh) saying anything about "destroying the temple." The witnesses at his trial said that Jesus (pbuh) said "HE" will destroy it and raise it again. In John, Jesus (pbuh) never said who will actually destroy the temple. At any rate, Jesus (pbuh) is speaking of his body being destroyed as a temple and "it", his physical body, will be raised again. This agrees perfectly with Jesus (pbuh) going through this great ordeal and him being resuscitated. If he was resurrected, he would not need his body raised.

As for the first prophecy pertaining to Jonah (pbuh), we have conflicting reports which we must attempt to reconcile. We could go with Mark and conclude that Jesus (pbuh) did not give a sign at all. We must remember that these gospels were not written together. They were written years apart, in different places, and to different audiences. So when Mark's reader came across these verses, he could only believe that Jesus (pbuh) offer them no sign.

Luke gives the prophecy with no timeline. Matthew is the only gospel with the actual prophecy and the timeline together as a sign to Jesus' (pbuh) opponents, yet he records Jesus (pbuh) speaking on a different occasion without the timetable. Out of five opportunities, the gospel authors only have Jesus (pbuh) mentioning time once. Thus, it is fair to assume that Jesus (pbuh) was not emphasizing the time factor of Jonah (pbuh) in the gigantic fish, because there was a group of people who knew absolutely nothing of the time factor. Of course, Jesus (pbuh) was not in his tomb for three days and three nights at any rate. He was in the tomb Friday night before the Sabbath, Saturday morning, and Saturday night. Sunday morning, Mary came to the tomb and Jesus (pbuh) was gone (John 20:1-2). That is not 3 days and 3 nights, but 1 day and 2 nights. Actually when the guard was placed at the tomb, the gospel record doesn't say that he nor the chief priest and Pharisees looked in the sepulcher, thus Jesus (pbuh) could have escaped on Friday. This again dismisses the idea of 3 days and 3 nights.

Some Christians suggest that the three days and three nights were not to be taken literally as 72 hours. They claim that in the Bible it means any part of three days, which I hold no objection to, despite there being only two days in which Jesus (pbuh) was entombed. What I object to is the idea that a time factor is a sign from heaven at all. The time is what some believe Jesus (pbuh) was emphasizing with the prophecy of Jonah (pbuh). I can do anything for three days and three nights or part of three days and it is not construed as a sign from heaven. Everyone on earth has done something for three days and it is not taken as a sign from

God. Not to mention, Jesus (pbuh) apparently did not tell everyone about the time factor. The people in which he gave the sign of Jonah (pbuh) without the timeline were left ignorant of the "three days and three nights" as a sign from heaven. So, it's obvious that the time was not the sign from heaven, but what happened in that time period was the sign. The sign of Jonah (pbuh) is the same as the sign of the destroyed temple. The timeline is incidental. We have three of the gospels which speak of the sign of Jonah (pbuh). In them Jesus (pbuh) is saying as Jonah (pbuh) "WAS" so shall he "BE."

THE STORY OF JONAH (pbuh)

Jonah (pbuh) was told by God to go to a place called Nineveh to warn the people that their sins were drawing God's notice. However, Jonah (pbuh) fled to Tarshish by way of ship. Because Jonah (pbuh) was abandoning his duty, God caused a great wind to disrupt his travels. Those on the ship with Jonah (pbuh) feared for their lives, so they prayed to their God and they cast lots to determine which person on the ship was responsible for the tumultuous ride. They determine that it was Jonah (pbuh), who had invoked the punishment of God on the ship. Jonah (pbuh) confessed to disobeying God's command and he requested his shipmates to throw him overboard in order to calm the waters. It is unclear why he did not simply jump himself, because he was now possibly causing his shipmates to be implicated in his murder. Because of this possibility, they all accepted Jonah's (pbuh) God and they are literally begging God not to punish them for their actions.

Jonah 1:14 _Wherefore they cried unto HaShem, and said: 'We beseech Thee, O HaShem, we beseech Thee, let us not perish for this man's life, and lay not upon us innocent blood; for Thou, O HaShem, hast done as it_ *pleased Thee.'*

Jonah 1:15 *So they took up Jonah, and cast him forth into the sea; and the sea ceased from its raging.*

Jonah 1:16 *Then the men feared HaShem exceedingly; and they offered a sacrifice unto HaShem, and made vows*

Jonah 2:1 *And HaShem prepared a great fish to swallow up*

Jonah; and Jonah was in the belly of the fish three days and three nights.

Jonah 2:2 *Then Jonah prayed unto HaShem his G-d out of the fish's belly.*

Jonah 2:3 *And he said: I called out of mine affliction unto HaShem, and He answered me; out of the belly of the nether-world cried I, and Thou heardest my voice.*

At this point, we must ask ourselves before Jonah (pbuh) is thrown into the water, was he dead? Was Jonah (pbuh) dead inside of the gigantic fish? And finally was he dead when he was vomited by the gigantic fish back onto shore? The answer is no, no, and no. Jonah (pbuh) volunteered to be thrown into the water, so he is ALIVE (Jonah 1:12). When the fish shallows him, Jonah (pbuh) prayed inside the gigantic fish, so he is ALIVE (Jonah 2:2). When Jonah (pbuh) was vomited onto the shore, God commanded him a second time to deliver his message, so he was ALIVE (Jonah 2:11-3:3).

THIS is a sign from heaven. A man is supposed to die, but he does not. This is what Jesus (pbuh) was speaking of when he said "as Jonas (pbuh) was three days and three nights in the gigantic fish's belly; so shall the Son of man be three days and three nights in the heart of the earth." The sign is not the time at all. In fact, the time Jonah (pbuh) spent inside the gigantic fish is of little significance without Jonah (pbuh) being ALIVE. The survival was the "sign of Jonah (pbuh)."

Yet Christians boast that Jesus (pbuh) was DEAD before he went into the tomb, he was DEAD while inside the tomb and he was RESURRECTED when he came out of the tomb. All of these things make Jesus totally UNLIKE Jonah (pbuh) in the belly of the gigantic fish. For Jesus' (pbuh) prophecy to be fulfilled, you must agree with me that Jesus (pbuh) was ALIVE when he came off of the cross, ALIVE when he went into the tomb, ALIVE inside of the tomb and ALIVE when he came out.

There are more details of the story of Jonah (pbuh) which are very interesting. There are great parallels to be drawn from the story of Jonah (pbuh) and that of Jesus (pbuh). One of them is similarities between the shipmates and Pontius Pilate and the centurion. These two parties have some culpability in the death of the two prophets, yet they wish to be cleared of any wrongdoing to an innocent man. Both of them send their respective prophets to their apparent death. One might also wonder if Jesus (pbuh) prayed to God to be delivered from his affliction inside the tomb as Jonah (pbuh) prayed to God inside the gigantic fish. We know that Jesus (pbuh) prayed for salvation before his capture, so prayer in the tomb is a possibility, especially if Jesus (pbuh) is like Jonah (pbuh). Also noteworthy is the confirmation in Jonah's (pbuh) prayers that God "hearing" prayers and God "answering" prayers are used synonymously in the Bible (Jonah 2:3). So Jesus' (pbuh) prayers were heard and answered as Jonah's (pbuh) were. Another point to be made is that there was little distinction between the two men's message to their people. Jonah's (pbuh) mission was to tell his people to repent from their evil ways (Jonah 1:2) as Jesus (pbuh) told to his people. The difference was Jesus' (pbuh) people rejected his message and Jonah's (pbuh) people accepted his message. The people repented of their sins and changed their ways and God forgave them, WITHOUT A SACRIFICE (Jonah 3:10).

So the Jews, Pharisees, Sadducees and scribes were told by Jesus (pbuh) of this sign of Jonah (pbuh), so why didn't Jesus (pbuh) ever show them their sign according to the gospels? The sign they asked for was to help them to believe in Jesus (pbuh). It was obviously important to them and to Jesus (pbuh), since he spoke of it on at least 3 different occasions. The problem was that Jesus (pbuh) was not resurrected. A resurrected being cannot die anymore. Jesus (pbuh) was ALIVE and to remain that way he had to avoid his enemies. If Jesus (pbuh) was unable to be harmed, it makes absolutely no sense for Jesus (pbuh) not to show his enemies the sign he promised them. Of the hundreds of prophecies said to point to Jesus' (pbuh) crucifixion, Jesus' (pbuh) own prophecy of his survival of the crucifixion should be the most important.

DIE FOR A LIE

One argument used to authenticate the death and resurrection of Jesus (pbuh) was the disciples' willingness to be ridiculed, persecuted and killed because of their belief that Jesus (pbuh) died and was resurrected. Some Christians take opposition to the word "belief." Because the disciples saw and touched Jesus (pbuh), they reason that they did not believe, but they "knew" for a fact that Jesus (pbuh) died and was resurrected. The problem with this line of reasoning is now apparent. Jesus (pbuh) did not die on the cross and he was not resurrected, therefore the "die for a lie" argument only helps my case. They "knew" that Jesus (pbuh) was ALIVE and they proclaimed this fact and they were willing to die for this proclamation. In actuality, the early Christians were persecuted because they would not worship the emperor of Rome. They were persecuted because they would not deviate from the belief in monotheism, not because they thought that Jesus (pbuh) was resurrected from the dead.

Also Peter had been mocked, persecuted, beaten and imprisoned for propagating his faith, but his propagation excluded gentiles. He and all the other disciples were teaching that gentiles were unfit for Jesus' (pbuh) mission because they were not Jews, they ate unclean food and they were uncircumcised. And he was so convinced of this that he suffered repeated abuse to convey this message. Of course, later he was said to have seen a vision which rectified this view, but the problem is that he suffered punishment and he was willing to die for a lie. Actually the call to teach non-Jews was said to be delivered by the resurrected Jesus (pbuh) (Mark 16:15), yet the disciples were still confused. If the Bible asserts that the disciples were mistaken in who the mission was geared to, despite clear instructions, could they not be mistaken in other important points.

PAUL

I think that many people do not realize that Paul's works were merely letters to different people of different cities. Epistles simply means letters. I wonder if Paul ever thought that these letters would someday be held in such high regard and placed in the same binding with the Tanakh, in which he once placed all authority. Paul was a Jew and an early persecutor of Christians, until he said he saw a vision of Jesus (pbuh) and he was converted to Christianity. Paul began preaching Christianity to the gentiles and he wrote letters conveying his version of Christianity. It is true that there were many versions of Christianity after Jesus' (pbuh) death, but Paul's version became the most popular and his words became "the words of God" to most Christians. His letters shaped Christians' view of Jesus (pbuh), and his teaching even shaped Jesus' (pbuh) biographies.

Paul's heavy influence is the only logical reason why the gospels do not delve into the character of Jesus' (pbuh) closest friends, the twelve disciples. They would be the candidates most likely to convey Jesus' (pbuh) message accurately to others, but they are depicted in the gospels as followers who had a hard time understanding anything Jesus (pbuh) did or said. The gospels record Jesus (pbuh) ridiculing them throughout his time with them, despite their obvious importance to him and to the proclamation of his message.

Another person who was instrumental in the development of the early church was James, Jesus' (pbuh) brother, but the gospels say that he was hostile towards Jesus (pbuh). He even considered Jesus (pbuh) to be out of his mind (Mark 3:21), yet he became a great leader of the church shortly after Jesus' (pbuh) lifetime. And he became an author of a book of the New Testament. His drastic transformation and its explanation are nowhere to be found in the gospels. Mary Magdalene, Joseph and Nicodemus are figures that are paramount to Jesus' (pbuh) survival, yet there is very little written about them and how they gained favor with Jesus (pbuh). Perhaps Paul's influence encouraged the author of John to downplay the role of Jesus' (pbuh) mother as well. [Jesus (pbuh) addressed her as "woman" in the gospel.] These seemingly intentional omissions minimize the role of others to help illuminate the role of Paul, who was admittedly a very rude and boastful man. He was also an admitted thief.

__2Corinthians 11:6__ But though I be rude in speech, yet not in knowledge; but we have been throughly made manifest among you in all things.

__2Corinthians 11:7__ Have I committed an offence in abasing myself that ye might be exalted, because I have preached to you the gospel of God freely?

__2Corinthians 11:8__ I robbed other churches, taking wages of them, to do you service.

He reasons that taking from others for a good cause is acceptable. Did he get such guidance from God or from Jesus (pbuh)? Probably not, still he is the most prolific writer in all of the Bible. And his works helped shape the image of Jesus (pbuh) in the gospels. Despite Paul's influence, the message of Jesus (pbuh) can still be understood in the gospels, if you read the gospels without any preconceived notions. But most people go into their reading with the words of Paul in mind.

1Corinthians 15:14 *And if Christ be not risen, then is our preaching vain, and your faith is also vain.*

In this letter to the Corinthians, Paul singled-handedly dismantled the entire message of Jesus (pbuh). In one chapter and one verse, everything Jesus (pbuh) taught was rendered irrelevant if he was not raised from the dead. Without this event, every action and every belief of the Christian is useless. Now Jesus' (pbuh) death has to be of the utmost importance to them. When a Christian reads the gospel accounts with mountains of evidence against the death and resurrection of Jesus (pbuh) as a price for sin, it doesn't register to him. It can't, unless he is willing to concede that his faith and preaching are in vain. All that they can see is "he gave up the ghost."

Whether Paul intentional altered Jesus' (pbuh) teaching is impossible to know. All I can do is state that he definitely did alter them. Jesus (pbuh), in no way, said everything hinges on his death or his resurrected. EVER. Paul's very own conversion is heaped in controversy. The book of Acts mentions it on three different occasions with differing details every time (Acts 9:4-9, 22:7-11, 26:13-16). And many of his methods and writings are questionable. He is recorded as saying some of his works in the Bible are his own opinion and not God's words (1Cor. 7:25-26, 2Cor. 11:17). Paul also admits to using trickery to gain converts (2Cor. 12:16, Romans 3:7). Is this the man to listen to over Jesus (pbuh)?

It is Paul who says Jesus (pbuh) was the Passover lamb (1Cor. 5:7-8). This was a lamb slaughtered by the Jews when they were enslaved by the Egyptians. The blood of the lamb was put over the door of the Israelites, so when the Lord came he would pass over their homes and go to the home of the Egyptians and kill their firstborn child.

Exodus 12:29 *And it came to pass at midnight, that HaShem smote all the firstborn in the land of Egypt, from the first-born of Pharaoh that sat on his throne unto the first-born of the captive that was in the dungeon; and all the first-born of cattle.*

The fact that Paul endorses such a heinous act is grounds to dismiss his authority. It is impossible to believe a just God would kill innocent children in order to persuade the pharaoh to release the Israelites. I guess this kind of belief could easily formulate into a belief in the murder of an innocent man to take away the sins of the guilty. Also difficult to believe is the notion that God cannot distinction between the Israelites and Egyptians without blood over their door. But even if this story is believed to be true, it would mean that Paul is declaring that Jesus (pbuh) only came to save the JEWS. The slaughter of the lamb was in no way a means of hope for the Egyptians. If they were to have the blood placed on their door, their children's salvation would have been accidental. On this occasion Paul hurts his own cause.

And we must remember that Jesus (pbuh) strongly emphasized the adherence to the laws of Moses (pbuh). He said you must follow the laws down to the smallest letter. However, Paul is one of those who teach men not to follow the laws of Moses (pbuh), which places him in direct opposition to Jesus (pbuh). Paul says you can be righteous without the laws (Romans 3:20-24). Paul says the law is nailed to the cross (Col. 2:13-14). He maintains that Christians are no longer under the tutelage of the laws (Gal. 3:24-25). He says Jesus (pbuh) abolished the laws (Eph. 2:15). It is Paul who dismisses God's EVERLASTING covenant with his people (Gen. 17:13-14).

Galatians 5:2 *Behold, I Paul say unto you, that if ye be circumcised, Christ shall profit you nothing.*

Galatians 5:3 _For I testify again to every man that is circumcised, that he is a debtor to do the whole law._

This bold declaration by Paul is completely against the teachings of Jesus (pbuh). Paul says that Jesus' (pbuh) entire life is worthless to them, if they are merely circumcised. This seems to be a blatant move to have Christians violate an extremely important covenant made with God and his followers. A covenant in which Paul himself, all the disciples and Jesus (pbuh) had partaken in as Jews. Cleverly, Paul makes the consequence for circumcision to be that the person must now follow all the laws of Moses (pbuh), a criteria that Jesus (pbuh) had already articulated whether you are circumcised or not. So Paul creates the dilemma of choosing the easy way of simply believing in Jesus' (pbuh) death and resurrection or taking the difficult road and following all the laws of Moses (pbuh). We must remember that Jesus (pbuh) said that the way to destruction is the EASY way and the way to heaven is the narrow or hard way (Matthew 17:13-14). The beloved disciple of Jesus (pbuh), John, attests to his master's words.

1John 5:3 _For this is the love of God, that we keep his commandments: and his commandments are not grievous._

Paul says anyone following the laws is under a curse (Gal. 3:10). And because the Jewish Torah says that any man hanged is accursed, Jesus (pbuh) is also cursed. Paul, realizing the implications of his words, accepts the premise that Jesus (pbuh) is cursed, but that Jesus (pbuh) made himself a curse for us. Paul attempts to make this curse something noble, however the stipulations in the Jewish Torah are that the person hung has "committed a SIN worthy of death and he be put to death" (Deut. 21:22-23). Of course, we now see that Jesus (pbuh) was not put to death, but are Christians willing to concede that Jesus (pbuh) committed a sin worthy of death?

Without speculating on his sincerity, it is obvious that the vision that Paul saw to cause his conversion was not actually Jesus (pbuh), unless Jesus (pbuh) decided to render every word he uttered in his lifetime to be of no further importance. And this is the situation the Christians are in today. When confronted with the words of Jesus (pbuh), they retaliate with the words of Paul. If the two arguments can't be reconciled, then Paul is wrong, automatically. But Christianity's doctrines come from Paul's teaching. He is the real founder of Christianity. Paul says the root of Christianity is not in Jesus' (pbuh) teachings at all, but in his resurrection. Without this there is no Christianity. Yet Paul gives a different account of Jesus' (pbuh) resurrection than that of the gospels.

1Corinthians 15:3 For I delivered unto you first of all that which I also received, how that Christ died for our sins according to the scriptures;

1Corinthians 15:4 And that he was buried, and that he rose again the third day according to the scriptures:

1Corinthians 15:5 And that he was seen of Cephas, then of the twelve:

1Corinthians 15:6 After that, he was seen of above five hundred brethren at once; of whom the greater part remain unto this present, but some are fallen asleep.

You will notice Paul's interpretation of Jesus' (pbuh) supposed death was as a sacrifice for everyone, a sentiment adopted by the gospel writers. Also Paul says Jesus (pbuh) was seen of Peter, but he makes no mention of Mary Magdalene (Mark 16:9), who saw Jesus (pbuh) first and then she informed Peter (Cephas). And if Peter is excluded, who are the 12 disciples? Judas is reported to be dead, when Jesus (pbuh) appeared to the disciples (Matt. 27:5). That makes 10 disciples. Perhaps Paul was adding Joseph of Arthimaea, a secret disciple. The problem is the gospels do not say this. The gospels speak of Jesus (pbuh) appearing to two disciples (Mark 16:12), then to all ELEVEN (Matt. 28:16, Mark 16:14, Luke 24:33). However John says that there were 11 disciples who saw Jesus (pbuh). And one disciple, Thomas, did not see him (John 20:24). The synoptic gospels say 11, John says 12 and Paul says 13. Which one is right?

Paul also says that Jesus (pbuh) appeared to over 500 of his brethren. There is no evidence of this in the gospels. Did the biographers, which were allegedly two disciples, forget that Jesus (pbuh) appears to over 500 people? And in view of the importance of this event in Christianity, it is amazing that Paul makes absolutely no mention of an empty tomb. But Paul does agree with the disciples that Jesus (pbuh) did not appear to his enemies, but to his disciples and brethren. Why not? Could they have killed him again? The answer to this question is probably the greatest difference between the gospel account of the resurrection and that taught by Paul.

1Corinthians 15:42 So also is the resurrection of the dead. It is sown in corruption; it is raised in incorruption:

1Corinthians 15:43 It is sown in dishonour; it is raised in glory: it is sown in weakness; it is raised in power:

1Corinthians 15:44 It is sown a natural body; it is raised a spiritual body. There is a natural body, and there is a spiritual body.

Paul agrees with Jesus (pbuh) that a resurrected body is a spiritual body. It has no weaknesses and it can no longer die. The huge problem Paul has, is that Jesus (pbuh) was not a spiritual being, but a physical being according to the gospels, where Jesus (pbuh) clearly said he was not a spirit. He had flesh and bones and he ate food. He even had the wounds from this ordeal which Thomas touched. Paul's description of Jesus (pbuh) after his supposed death also contradicts the apologist's notion that Jesus (pbuh) was a spiritual being with a physical body. And it helps to solidify my claim that Jesus (pbuh) was ALIVE. The crowning jewel is delivered by the Gospel writer Luke in the Book of Acts. He corroborates my explanation explicitly.

Acts 1:3 After his suffering, he presented himself to them and gave many convincing proofs that he was ALIVE....Acts 1:9 After he said this, he was taken up before their very eyes, and a cloud hid him from their sight.

Luke, here, says that Jesus (pbuh) gave "convincing proofs" that he was ALIVE. From the eating of the broiled fish, to his disguise, to his several appearances, to Thomas touching him, they were all "proofs" that he was ALIVE. Luke supports my usage of these events as compelling evidence that he had survived his ordeal. And notice that Luke says "after his suffering," not "after his death." These verses above carry almost the exact same meaning as the verses of the Qur'an which says Jesus (pbuh) was not killed or crucified, but God raised him to himself. That such verses exist in the Bible is amazing.

Paul misrepresentation of Jesus (pbuh) is the foundation of Christianity. It is Paul who deemed that man is saved by faith in Jesus' (pbuh) death and resurrection, not works (Eph. 2:8-9). Jesus (pbuh) taught belief in him as a servant of God. And as a servant of God he asked man to do good works. It is faith AND works which Jesus (pbuh) taught. James summed it up superbly when he wrote

James 2:17 Even so faith, if it hath not works, is dead, being alone.

James 2:18 *Yea, a man may say, Thou hast faith, and I have works: shew me thy faith without thy works, and I will shew thee my faith by my works.*

James 2:19 *Thou believest that there is one God; thou doest well: the devils also believe, and tremble.*

James 2:20 *But wilt thou know, O vain man, that faith without works is dead?*

CHAPTER IX – ISLAM

Al-Qur'an 13:29

"For those who believe and work righteousness, is (every)

blessedness, and a beautiful place of (final) return."

With respect to James, it is God who sums it up best when explaining the path to Paradise. In the book of Exodus (32:33) there is reference to the Book of God. This is not actually a book, but it is the knowledge of God of all things. Does he have this book or knowledge for naught? No. It is a record of all man's actions and intentions and this is what man will be judged by on the last day which Jesus (pbuh) spoke of. If our actions and intentions are not rewarded or punished, then the knowledge of them, in pursuit of justice, is in vain. In Islam, you will be reward or punished for EVERY action and intention you have done. There is no one who will bear your sins for you. You bear the punishment for your own sin, unless you repent for it. This is why it is important to be like the Prodigal son and return, repent, reject your sins and make compensation if possible to those you have wronged. Only you and God know your level of sincerity in your repentance. But you are rewarded for every action with its intention.

In Islam, the elder son in the story of the Prodigal son will be given more rewards for his higher level of obedience. In Luke's gospel, Jesus (pbuh) speaks of the angels of heaven being more joyful over the repentance of one sinner, than they are for the constant obedience of God's servants (15:7, 10). This notion seems to encourage disobedience followed by repentance over perpetual devotion. On the contrary, Islam has ranks and levels in heaven based upon your righteousness. The more righteous you are, the better your reward. And based upon your wickedness, you are punished more or less severely, as well. Is this not justice? Should the sinless person be rewarded the same as a person who has yesterday decide to live righteously?

Islam means submission to the will of God and a Muslim is one who submits his will to God. In order to submit your will to God, you have to be a believer in God to some degree. The degree to which you believe is the degree to which you will submit to God. So belief and works make you a Muslim. When Jesus (pbuh) said, "not as I will, but as you (God) will" (Luke 22:42), he personified the perfect Muslim and the perfect believer when he forsook his own will for God's will. There are billions of people today who believe in God. The problem is that they do not know what his will is. If you are following the book of a man about God, you are actually following the will of that man, not of God. And this is what has happened in religions around the world. The emphasis is on man and not on God.

Islam has the book of God, the Qur'an. In it is the true will of God revealed to Muhammad (pbuh). Jesus, Moses, Abraham, Isaac and Ishmael (pbut) all received inspiration from God and they all taught the true will of God. But throughout history, their message has been altered. Jesus' (pbuh) case is the most concisely proven in this book. He is said to have preached the gospel, but his gospel is not to be found anywhere. In the biographies of his life, we get some of the message of Jesus (pbuh), but not the actual words of God to Jesus. Fortunately, we do have the words of God to Muhammad (pbuh) in the Qur'an.

It may come to the surprise of many, but Muhammad was foretold in the Bible by Jesus (pbut). The gospels also confirm that the Jews were expecting Muhammad (pbuh). When they came to John the Baptist, they asked him, was he Elijah (pbut)? And he said no. They asked was he the Christ? And he said no. And they asked him was he THAT PROPHET? And he said no (John 1:20-21). Now we know that Jesus was the Christ and according to Jesus, John was Elijah, so who was THAT prophet (pbut)? "That prophet" was the prophet foretold by Moses (pbuh), who would be like Moses (pbuh). Without getting into details, we can see that the Jews were looking for three people. WHO WAS THE THIRD PERSON? If we put the list in order, Elijah was to come before the Christ, and after the Christ was "that prophet" (pbut).

The only person Jesus (pbuh) spoke of coming after him was "the Comforter." Christians quickly point out that the Comforter is the Holy Spirit (John 14:26). However Jesus (pbuh) described this person as "another" Comforter and he will complete Jesus' (pbuh) mission (John 14:16, John 16:7-14). Jesus (pbuh) was the first Comforter, so who was the second Comforter. The Greek word for "another" in this place, "heteros" means "of the same nature." Jesus (pbuh) is saying that the next Comforter will be just like him, of the same nature. If Jesus (pbuh) is the first Comforter and the second Comforter is a spirit, it would not be of the same nature as Jesus (pbuh), would it? Jesus (pbuh) is speaking of a PERSON with a holy spirit, not the actual Holy Spirit. Jesus (pbuh) uses 7 masculine pronouns in this one verse to describe the Comforter to illustrate that he is speaking of a MAN, not a spirit.

John 16:13 Howbeit when he, the Spirit of truth, is come, he will guide you into all truth: for he shall not speak of himself; but whatsoever he shall hear, [that] shall he speak: and he will show you things to come.

If he were speaking of a spirit, he would have used the word "it." Also, the author of this gospel uses the word prophet and spirit synonymously.

1John 4:1 _Beloved, believe not every spirit, but try the spirits whether they are of God: because many false prophets are gone out into the world._

Therefore every true prophet is a true spirit and every holy prophet is a holy spirit. Another reason we can determine that Jesus (pbuh) is not speaking of the Holy Spirit is that the Comforters terms of arrival was conditional (John 16:7), whereas the Holy Spirit was here at the beginning of creation (Gen 1:2), it was with John the Baptist's (pbuh) parents (Luke 1:41, 1:67), and with Jesus (pbuh). Not to mention, the Holy Spirit was helping the disciples in their preaching and Jesus (pbuh) gave the Holy Spirit to them after the "crucifiction" (John 20:22), long before the Day of Pentecost (This word is courtesy of Ahmed Deedat, who also provided the explanation for the Comforter. He suggested that "Crucifiction" should be in the English dictionary as a word used for someone who is hung on a cross, but is not killed). Jesus (pbuh) said if he doesn't leave, then the Comforter will not come, so he definitely could not have been speaking of the Holy Spirit because the Holy Spirit was there all the time.

This Comforter is called the "spirit of truth." The Prophet Muhammad (pbuh) was called "Al-Amin," the truthful. (He was so truthful that when he said he received revelation from God, the people of Mecca knowing that he never lied, initially assumed that he had gone mad). This spirit or prophet of truth "shall not speak of himself; but whatsoever he shall hear, that shall he speak" (John 16:13). Again this prophecy is fitting Muhammad (pbuh) like a glove. The Qur'an is believed to be the direct revelation given to Prophet Muhammad (pbuh) by an angel of God. The angel gave him the words of God and he spoke them, often times in direct response to a question or situation that arouse.

And this Comforter will guide you into ALL truth (John 16:13). All the truth that Jesus (pbuh) spoke of is Islam. Jesus (pbuh) said he has many things to say, but he was unable to. The Qur'an confirms that Jesus (pbuh) brought SOME of the truth (43:63). This is because he was constantly on the run. For as much love as Jesus (pbuh) received, there was also a hatred for him and a need to silence him. His enemies sought every opportunity to discredit him, ridicule him and kill him. Under these circumstances, it is obvious that Jesus (pbuh) could not deliver his message thoroughly. His successor, the Comforter, would convey ALL OF THE TRUTH. The Christian's concept of the Holy Spirit is incapable of giving you all truth. When Christians get the Holy Spirit in them, it is a FEELING that they get, just as the people of Pentecost got from the Holy Spirit (Acts 2:1-4). This spirit does not explain doctrine or answer inquiries. It can inspire you and convince you that you are on the right path, but throughout the Bible, it is man who delivers truth to the rest of humanity. The Comforter is a man who delivers the truth. And if Jesus (pbuh) brought some truth and the Comforter brought all of the truth, then we can deduce that as Jesus (pbuh) was the way to God, so too was the Comforter "the way, the truth and the life."

Also Jesus said that John the Baptist was the greatest man to ever live, because he was the predecessor to Jesus (pbut). Yet Jesus said that he is greater than John the Baptist (pbut) (John 5:36). Now what does that say about the greatness of Jesus' (pbuh) successor, the Comforter?

John 14:16 *And his teachings will last forever.*

The Qur'an, which makes the claim to be the last revelation sent to mankind (the Bible does not make such a claim), has been unchanged since its inception. And it will last forever. It is Prophet Muhammad

147

(pbuh) who insists in the Qur'an that Jesus (pbuh) was not killed on the cross, not the HOLY SPIRIT. The Holy Spirit of the Christians has led them to believe that Jesus (pbuh) died for their sins, which is the furthest thing from the truth. It is clear that the Prophet Muhammad (pbuh) has met the criteria of being the Comforter more so than the Holy Spirit.

Because of the Jews' constant rejection of Jesus (pbuh) and other prophets, the responsibility to give God's message to others was passed to another people. The Comforter, Prophet Muhammad (pbuh), came from among the brethren of the Israelites, the Ishmaelite. It is a divine order by God, that if you do not fulfill your duties to God, he will substitute you with another people more fit to do the job, and "they won't be like you" (Al-Qur'an 47:38). And Jesus (pbuh) verifies this claim (Matt. 12:43, Mark 12:9).

JESUS ON THE CROSS?

It is interesting to note that Jesus (pbuh), when speaking of the Comforter, says if "I go away" and "if I depart" then he will come (John 16:7). This is not the words used to describe your death and there is absolutely no "if" when discussing your death, it's "when." What does "go away" and "depart" mean? The Qur'an says that Jesus (pbuh) was neither "killed nor crucified." That is to say, he was not hung on a cross at all.

Al-Qur'an 4:157

That they said (in boast), "We killed Christ Jesus the son of Mary, the Messenger of Allah";- but they killed him not, nor crucified him, but so it was made to appear to them, and those who differ therein are full of doubts, with no (certain) knowledge, but only conjecture to follow, for of a surety they killed him not:-

<u>Al-Qur'an 4:158</u>

Nay, Allah raised him up unto Himself; and Allah is Exalted in Power, Wise

What Jesus (pbuh) meant, when he said he was departing and going away, was that he will be saved and raised to God. The writers of the Gospels construed this as Jesus (pbuh) saying he was going to be killed and they put these words into his mouth on occasion. The Qur'an says God delivered Jesus (pbuh) from the hands of his enemies just as the Psalms suggests.

<u>Psalms 34:20</u> *Many are the ills of the righteous, but Lord delivereth him out of them ALL.*

All ills would include the spitting, the beating, and the mocking from the soldiers. Even carrying the cross might be a burden Jesus (pbuh) did not have to bear. One gospel says Jesus (pbuh) did not carry the cross at all but Simon did. This is the same gospel which spoke of a suspicious naked man, perhaps hinting at a mistaken identity, because the person crucified was to be stripped of his clothes (Mark 15:24). God delivering Jesus (pbuh) from ALL ills would definitely include the nailing on a cross. And again Psalms comes to the rescue to show that Jesus (pbuh) was not crucified or affixed to a cross because it says he had no bones broken (Psalms 34:19). It is IMPOSSIBLE to not break any bones of a person who is nailed in his hands or wrists and feet to a cross. Muslim propagators Abdullah Smith and Ozzy of the <u>www.answering-christianity.com</u> website have found further proof that Jesus (pbuh) was saved from ALL ills.

The Psalms was quoted by the devil when tempting Jesus (pbuh). The devil asked Jesus (pbuh) to jump off of the top of the temple in Jerusalem. The devil reasoned that God would save Jesus (pbuh) from death "for it is written: 'He will command his angels concerning you, to guard you, and: With their hands they will support you, lest you dash your foot against a stone.'" (Luke 4:9-12). You see, it is foretold that God would spare Jesus (pbuh) from harm. But the true importance of this quotation is again realized when we go back to the original source. Psalms 91:11-12 is being quoted. Let us have a closer look.

Psalms 91:1 _You who dwell in the shelter of the Most High, who abide in the shadow of the Almighty,_

Psalms 91:2 _Say to the LORD, "My refuge and fortress, my God in whom I trust."_

Psalms 91:3 _God will rescue you from the fowler's snare, from the destroying plague,_

Psalms 91:4 _Will shelter you with pinions, spread wings that you may take refuge; God's faithfulness is a protecting shield._

Psalms 91:5 _You shall not fear the terror of the night nor the arrow that flies by day,_

Psalms 91:6 _Nor the pestilence that roams in darkness, nor the plague that ravages at noon._

Psalms 91:7 _Though a thousand fall at your side, ten thousand at your right hand, near you it shall not come._

Psalms 91:8 _You need simply watch; the punishment of the wicked you will see._

Psalms 91:9 _You have the LORD for your refuge; you have made the Most High your stronghold._

Psalms 91:10 No evil shall befall you, no affliction come near your tent.

Psalms 91:11 For God commands the angels to guard you in all your ways.

Psalms 91:12 With their hands they shall support you, lest you strike your foot against a stone.

Psalms 91:13 You shall tread upon the asp and the viper, trample the lion and the dragon.

Psalms 91:14 Whoever clings to me I will deliver; whoever knows my name I will set on high.

Psalms 91:15 All who call upon me I will answer; I will be with them in distress; I will deliver them and give them honor.

Psalms 91:16 With length of days I will satisfy them and show them my saving power.

This chapter is a hidden treasure. Like John's quotation of Psalms, it is a confirmation of the Muslim's belief. It is a miracle that such remnants of proof still exists in an ocean of detail of Jesus' (pbuh) alleged death. In this short verse is confirmation that God sent angels (at least three angel appearances within days of each other) "TO GUARD (HIM) IN ALL WAYS, and to save Jesus (pbuh) from all evil and all affliction, not so much as his foot will be wounded. Jesus (pbuh) called upon God with every fiber of his being and God heard and answered his prayer. God delivered him, showing his saving power. And there are many more prophecies attributed to Jesus (pbuh) which corroborate the Muslims' belief about Jesus' (pbuh) ordeal.

Psalms 3:4 To the LORD I cry aloud, and he answers me from his holy hill.

Psalms 18:6 In my distress I called to the LORD; I cried to my God for help. From his temple he heard my voice; my cry came before him, into his ears...*Psalms 18:16* He reached down from on high and took hold of me; he drew me out of deep waters. *Psalms 18:17* He rescued me from my powerful enemy, from my foes, who were too strong for me.

Psalms 138:7 Though I walk in the midst of trouble, you preserve my life; you stretch out your hand against the anger of my foes, with your right hand you save me.

Hosea 6:1 "Come, let us return to the LORD. He has torn us to pieces but he will heal us; he has injured us but he will bind up our wounds.

Hosea 6:2 After two days he will revive us; on the third day he will restore us, that we may live in his presence.

JESUS BARABBAS AND A SUBSTITUTE

What is extremely odd is that the man released by Pontius Pilate and the crowd, Barabbas, was actually named Jesus Barabbas (Matthew 27:17). Some early Syriac manuscripts of Matthew present Barabbas' name twice as Jesus bar Abbas: manuscripts in the Caesarean text-type-the Sinaitic Palimpsest, the Syriac lectionaries and some of the manuscripts used by Origen in the 3rd century-all support Barabbas' name as Jesus Barabbas, though not all modern New Testament translations reflect this {http://www.answers.com/topic/barabbas}.

Barabbas literally means "son of the father" in Aramaic as it was probably used as a description similar to Jesus the Christ or Jesus the son of God. So this man was "Jesus son of the Father." It is well-documented throughout the gospels that Jesus (pbuh) called God "Father" and he uses the terms, God and Father, interchangeably. Is it a coincidence that this criminal has the same name as Jesus (pbuh) and is called by a similar title? Perhaps amongst the many mistakes of the authors, one was that they did not realize that the Jesus who was chosen by the crowd was the wrong Jesus and they actually crucified the man that committed some heinous crimes.

__John 19:5__ When Jesus came out wearing the crown of thorns and the purple robe, Pilate said to them, "Here is the man!"

Which man? Which Jesus? With the crown of thorns causing the man to bleed down his face, and Pilate's announcement, it seems as though Pilate is identifying him to the crowd. Pilate knew that a grave injustice was being perpetrated, would he not substitute a criminal for an innocent man? There have long been people who held the belief that Jesus (pbuh) was not crucified, but that he was substituted with someone else. One on the gospels which was left out of the Bible was called the "Gospel of Barnabas." This gospel maintains that Judas was crucified in place of Jesus (pbuh). Some early Christians thought it was Simon of Cyrene, the man who carried the cross for Jesus (pbuh). Other early Christians like the Basilidians, the Carpocratians believed that it was not Jesus (pbuh), but someone resembling him that was crucified (The Basilidians also reject the divinity of Jesus). The Docetists and the Cerinthians were also early Christian groups who denied the crucifixion. This shows that Jesus' (pbuh) death has long been in dispute and this dispute was not from those who were against Jesus (pbuh), but those who purported to be his followers. They were not under the impression that without Jesus' (pbuh) death and resurrection their entire faith was in vain as Paul asserted in his letter to the Corinthians (1Cor. 15:14).

"... among early Christians, there was no commonly accepted meaning and understanding of the death of Jesus."

-Rev. Howard Bess

This is extremely important. There were early Christians who did not give meaning to his death and others who did not believe that he was crucified at all. This means that belief in his death and resurrection was not required amongst his early followers. It was made a requirement at a later date. Someone DECIDED to make this paramount for acceptance in Jesus (pbuh), just as people DECIDED that he was God, long after he was gone.

I must emphasize that the Qur'an does not say that Jesus (pbuh) was substituted. This is my own speculation, in light of the evidence presented from the Bible to establish that he was not killed on the cross. The Qur'an says Jesus (pbuh) was taken up by God. God saved Jesus (pbuh) from this excruciating and humiliating death. So Jesus (pbuh) was not resurrected from death, but rescued from death and his ascension was God taking him up to heaven. All the gospels agree that Jesus (pbuh) did ascend to heaven except Matthew. He makes no mention of it, probably because as scholars say he copied Mark, whose gospel did not contain the verses about his resurrection or his ascension at that time.

Now the Qur'an says that evil men plan and God also plans and God is the best of planners (8:30). Some Christians have argued that because the Qur'an says it only appeared that Jesus (pbuh) was killed, this makes God a deceiver. This argument is an act of desperation. What is the problem with convincing criminals that they have killed someone, in order to free an innocent man? And the gospels are in agreement with the Qur'an as I have proven.

The Jews thought they kill Jesus (pbuh), but they did not. The Qur'an does not say, as some claim, that there was a substitute for Jesus (pbuh) or that the disciples were fooled. It only says that those who sought to kill him were mistaken. A Christian who makes this argument must explain why Jeremiah, a prophet of God, accused God of DECEIVING him (Jer. 20:7). They must also consider Paul's testimony.

2Thessalonians 2:11 *And for this cause God shall send them strong delusion, that they should believe a lie*

SLEW AND HANGED ON A TREE

While making the finishing touches to this book, I stumbled across a debate on the subject of Jesus' (pbuh) resurrection between David Wood, a Christian and Shadid Lewis, a Muslim. I was surprise to recognize Shadid Lewis as a Muslim that I had met once and whom I had just written about in my book "Islam is the Truth" on the subject of war. In any case, Shadid mentioned many of the points that I have written here. And one point that he made in particular was rather remarkable. He suggested that the Bible contains two depictions of the crucifixion of Jesus (pbuh). The first is the most popular crucifixion of the Romans which I have discussed thus far. The second is the crucifixion described in the book of Acts. In Acts 5:30 and 10:39 the disciples accuse the JEWS of killing Jesus (pbuh).

Acts 5:30 *The God of our fathers raised up Jesus, whom you slew and hanged on a tree.*

Acts 10:39 *And we are witnesses of all things which he did both in the land of the Jews, and in Jerusalem; whom they slew and hanged on a tree*

The key to Shadid's assessment is the words "slew and hanged on a tree." These words are in reference to the punishment spoken of in the book of Deuteronomy.

Deut. 21:22 *And if a man have committed a sin worthy of death, and he be to be put to death, and thou hang him on a tree*

There are a few things that need to be pointed out. One thing is that the criminal is to be killed first and then hanged. The hanging is not the cause of death. The man is to be stoned to death and then hung on a tree as a means of humiliation. Notice in Acts, Jesus (pbuh) is slew AND hanged, though some translators have mistakenly substituted the words "and hanged" with the words "by hanging." Also he is to be hanged on a TREE. Both verses on Acts say Jesus (pbuh) was hanged to a TREE in accordance with their law in Deuteronomy and not the cross used by the Romans. Acts 13:29 also reiterates the point that Jesus was hung to a TREE.

In chapter 13, the Jews are asking Pilate for permission to be Jesus' (pbuh) executioner. This would make sense considering the disdain that the Jews had for Jesus (pbuh). It would also explain Pilate literally "washing his hands" of the case as a gesture of deferment of some culpability in the killing an innocent man. And last but not least, Paul proclaims that it was "the Jews who killed the Lord Jesus" (1Thess. 2:14-15). The fact that Jesus (pbuh) was taken down in adherence to the Jewish Sabbath is also indicative of Jewish involvement with the crucifiction. Not to mention the fact that executions inside the city of Jerusalem were prohibited by Jewish Law. This would explain why Jesus (pbuh) was to be crucified at Golgotha, outside of Jerusalem. But again, this is a requisite for Jewish execution. Why were oppressive Romans following Jewish laws to execute a Jewish man accused of sedition against their regime? Pontius Pilate found no fault with Jesus (pbuh), yet many of the Jewish people persisting in his condemnation. It stands to reason that he was set to be killed by the Jewish hierarchy.

The implications of Shadid's findings are astounding. It has been many Muslims' view that when the Qur'an says that the Jews tried to kill Jesus (pbuh) their indictment was as a result of their campaign to have him killed. However, now it can be said that the Qur'an was more than accurate in its accusations against the Jews of Jesus' (pbuh) time, as some parts of the Bible attribute them with direct responsibility in this case. Even more amazing is the new meaning that is given to the Quranic message that "they killed him not, nor crucified him." If this depiction of the crucifiction is true then the Qur'an is precisely worded to be in complete opposition to both steps of punishment prescribed in the book of Deuteronomy.

COMING CLOSER TO ISLAM

While on a Christian website, I came across the mention of an author by the name of Marcus Borg. He is probably best known for his book entitled "The Heart of Christianity." But the work which was in discussion was "JESUS: Uncovering the Life, Teachings and Relevance of a religious Revolutionary." The Christians who read this book seemed to be changed profoundly by it. He presented them with an entirely new image of Jesus (pbuh), which they never imagined. They cited quotes from this book which compelled me to go and buy it for myself. Upon reading this book, it became abundantly clear that Borg was in almost total agreement with everything I believe about Jesus (pbuh). This man who is a Christian scholar, that is, a scholar who is a Christian, is in agreement with a Muslim on Jesus (pbuh). Here are some of the points Borg makes in this book:

-Matthew and Luke copied Mark and the "Q" to compose their book pg.33

-90% of Mark is found in Matthew pg. 33

-2/3 of Mark is found in Luke pg.33

-Jesus (pbuh) was in the tomb "less than 48 hrs" pg.143

-Jesus (pbuh) only came for the Jews pg. 167,145-146

-Jesus' (pbuh) teaches aren't timeless pg. 167

-Without preconceived notions of Jesus (pbuh) dying for sins, one would never think about it when reading the gospels pg. 269-270

-Jesus (pbuh) was naked on the cross pg.271

-Crucifixion takes several days to cause death pg.271

-According to the gospels, Jesus (pbuh) did not die for the sins of the world pg.274

I mention this to show that there are those in the folds of Christianity who are beginning to question the traditional understanding of Jesus (pbuh). They are sincere Christians who have no motive but the pursuit of truth. When someone takes an objective look at the gospels, their conclusions lead them to truths already affirmed in a book revealed to "that prophet" "like (Moses)" who will lead mankind into "all truth."

AN INVITATION

With an exploration of Islam, you will find TRUTH. The truth of Jesus' (pbuh) birth, message and his life, the truth about Adam (pbuh) and Eve, the truth about the prophets of God and the truth about the origin of the universe and the origin of man. Islam provides the true purpose of life and the means to its ultimate goal. More importantly, Islam provides man with the truth of God, with God's actual words. Truth is not time bound, culture bound or bound to any race. Everyone on earth is invited to examine the message of God to man for him or herself. Won't you accept this invitation?

FOR MORE INFORMATION READ:

The Holy Bible (NKJV or RSV)

The Holy Qur'an by Muhammad Marmaduke Pickthall, or M. H. Shakir

The Noble Qur'an by Drs. Muhammad Taqiud Din Halali and Muhammad Muhsin Khan

Crucifixion or Cruci-fiction by Ahmed Deedat

Jesus: Uncovering the Life, Teachings, and Relevance of a Religious Revolutionary by Marcus Borg

The Myth of the Cross by Alhaj A. D. Ajijola

Early Christian Doctrine by J. N. D. Kelly

What was the sign of Jonah? by Ahmed Deedat

Who Moved the Stone? by Ahmed Deedat

Resurrection or Resuscitation? by Ahmed Deedat

Muhammed, the Natural Successor to Christ by Ahmed Deedat

The Passover Plot by Hugh Schonfield

Jesus, Interrupted by Bart Ehrman

ABOUT THE AUTHOR

Mr. Campbell was raised attending both the Christian Church and the Muslim Mosque. He was always inquisitive about religion. Around the age of 14, he decided that Islam was the path for him. However, he was rather secretive about his belief due to the negative perception many had of the religion. When Islam became the topic of any discussion, he maintained the Islamic sympathizer role as the son of a Muslim, while being careful not to be identified as a Muslim himself. The stigma surrounding Islam and Muslims only intensified throughout the years, but so too did his desire to announce to the world that ISLAM IS THE TRUTH. Throughout his life, he had engage others in discussions on religion and a little over three years ago he realized that the issues that were raised in debate and in dialogue were issues which warranted extensive details, evidence and explanations. Drawing from all the books, lectures, and debates he come in contact with, and all the talks with Muslims, Christians, Jews, Hindus, atheists and agnostics, he set out to write one book which would convince all of the truth about the God of the universe. This one book blossomed into eight books which are written with the primary goal of proving the validity of Islam. It is with his sincerest effort that he wrote these books, with the hope that all readers will set aside their preconceived ideas and have an open mind.

BOOKS BY THIS AUTHOR INCLUDE:

"ISLAM IS THE TRUTH"
"JESUS WAS NOT CRUCIFIED"
"THE JEWISH TORAH IS NOT THE WORD OF GOD"
"THERE IS NO TRINITY"
"25 MYTHS ABOUT ISLAM"
"GOD THE IRRESISTIBLE"
"FAQs ABOUT ISLAM"
"WHAT GOD SAYS ABOUT JESUS"

FOR INFORMATION ON PURCHASING THESE BOOKS LOG ON TO
WWW.ISLAMISTHETRUTH.ORG